The Government of God

Standing at the Threshold of Divine Presence

Collegium Books

Mark David Shaw

Government Series

Unless otherwise indicated all Scripture quotations are taken from *New American Standard Bible : 1995 update*. 1995. LaHabra, CA: The Lockman Foundation.

Some Scripture quotations are taken from the following:

The Holy Bible : King James Version. 1995 (electronic ed. of the 1769 edition of the 1611 Authorized Version.). Bellingham WA: Logos Research Systems, Inc.
The New King James Version. 1982 (Ps 34:2). Nashville: Thomas Nelson.
The Everyday Bible : New Century Version. 2005. Nashville, TN.: Thomas Nelson, Inc.

The Government of God
by Mark David Shaw

ISBN 978-0-9801865-2-9

Published by Collegium Books
410 Dakota Street W.
Cannon Falls, MN 55903

To reach us on the Internet:

www.collegiumbooks.com
www.collegiumbibleinstitute.com

The Government of God

Standing at the Threshold of Divine Presence

Psalm 65:4 How blessed is the one whom You choose and bring near to You To dwell in Your courts. We will be satisfied with the goodness of Your house, Your holy temple.

This Book is Dedicated To:

The servants of the government of our church. Thank you for your endless hours of service, your dedication, your taking hold of the vision upon which we function as a group. God bless you richly.

Richard Farm
Brandon Gatzke
Brian Snelling
Roseann Snelling
Susie Snelling

The production volunteer, Zachariah Schraufnagel. Thank you for all of your help, your long drives, and the number of hours you spent videotaping. God Bless you!

Dean and Cathy Gallups for your volunteer work on the Scholarship Fund Committee, your desire for the mission field and your dedication to the vision of this ministry. May God's hand be upon you!

To our Sudanese students:

Gabriel Deng
Santino Shangag
Kamen Makuer

May you all have such an impact on Sudan and the local Sudanese community, that Christ is forever glorified through your work. Thank you for your example of love for your people.

Acknowledgements

To King Jesus, who is the Head of the Church. Without Him, I can do nothing!

To my wife Kathryn who helped me to get my mind around and understand the calling of prophet both from a theological and attitudinal perspective. Without her help, I would not have been able to complete this book and I would never have understood the prophetic ministry.

To Susie Snelling whose tireless dedication to this body of work through her proofing and suggestions drove her to finish it, thank you! We gave you a challenge and you met it head on and succeeded in a timely manner.

To my four children Elisha, Raquel, Michael, and Mindy who endured the government of our home, thank you for your love, your uniqueness, and for putting up with the long hours of study that made this and other books possible.

Table of Contents

Introduction

> **Exodus 25:8-9** *"Let them construct a sanctuary for Me, that I may dwell among them. According to all that I am going to show you, as the pattern of the tabernacle and the pattern of all its furniture, just so you shall construct it."*

Can you imagine Moses adding to or taking away from the instructions of God with regard to His sanctuary? Can you imagine after altering those instructions that God would come and dwell in it? If you answered "no" to those two questions, then you have laid an argument for structuring the Church in the manner that God told us to construct it.

The truth is, all too often we see that we are not really serious in regard to the government of the Church. Why do you think God asked Moses to build a sanctuary that was a copy? Could it be that when God dwells in a place, there are certain necessary prerequisites with regard to its structure? Do we really want His presence in His Church? We know He dwells in us individually, but does He dwell in us corporately?

What would it look like if God were to dwell in us corporately? There is a reason why I am using this language. I am not talking about God dwelling in a building. I am speaking of God dwelling in a people. What evidence do we have that would give us an idea as to what it looks like for God to dwell in a people? Could we perhaps say "dwell with?" We know that God dwelled with the nation of Israel before their rebellion. We know that God dwelled with Adam and Eve before their rebellion.

It is my contention that when God dwells with a people miracles happen. When He does not, they are very rare or completely missing. I don't know about you, but I want the miraculous back in the Church. David, I think, had a special insight into the presence of God. He seemed to speak of it often, and seemed to desire that environment over even being King of Israel.

> *Psalm 84:10-12 For a day in Your courts is better than a thousand outside. I would rather stand at the threshold of the house of my God Than dwell in the tents of wickedness. For the LORD God is a sun and shield; The LORD gives grace and glory; No good thing does He withhold from those who walk uprightly. O LORD of hosts, How blessed is the man who trusts in You!*

I want the good things God has for the Church. *"No good thing does He withhold from those who walk uprightly."* When we structure our churches to function like a business, or a military, we are not trusting in the Lord. When we put our desire above the desire of our God, we are not walking uprightly.

The Hebrew word for "uprightly" is *tamiyn* and means to be complete. What does it mean to be complete? It means that you are missing nothing. It cannot be speaking of talent or gifts since all of these come from Him. It must mean that I am following the instructions of the Lord.

I want to take a moment and say that God shows up at churches many times and in many ways. I think it is a wonderful thing to experience. But aren't we starving for more? I want God's presence continuously. I want to walk with Him like Adam. I want

Him to go before me and lead the way as He did for Israel. Can't we expect this? Can't we have this? Oh, my heart cries for more! If I did not think there was more to be had, my heart would not cry for more. There is! There is more!

That is why I have written this book. I believe that man has designed the government of the Church rather than allowing God to be the King. I am not satisfied with any man's system. I want God's government. I want to arrange His Church so that He would want to be with us corporately. I believe that God has left a lot of evidence that shows us what He wants.

This is not meant to be a tirade against other ministries. I am not thinking along those lines. I think that many times things get twisted and changed many generations in the past. Then when we continue doing things the same way for long enough it starts to look like the right way of doing it. I believe in testing all things. Let us start by testing the government of God and bring ourselves back into divine order and provide an atmosphere where the Holy One would want to dwell.

> *Psalm 22:3-5 Yet You are holy, O You who are enthroned upon the praises of Israel. In You our fathers trusted; They trusted and You delivered them. To You they cried out and were delivered; In You they trusted and were not disappointed.*

Note the element of trust. I think when we look at the different structures of church government what we see is a result of a lack of trust. We cannot trust in people. People will fail us. God will not. We can put our whole trust upon God. You will have to ask yourself a very important question. *"Is Jesus capable of directing His Church?"* This is not a structure without human leadership. It will be a structure with leadership devoted to the direction of the King, Jesus.

From The Set Man To The Council

Chapter One

I need you for a moment to take a step out of time in order to make sense of the movement of God. Why should we step out of time? It is necessary to measure God's movement by millennium since God is timeless and He has always been and will always be. This is hard to conceptualize because we have been conditioned to our surroundings by the passing of time at the same rate of speed for the whole of our life. Everything that we interact with through our senses has a beginning and an end. We see nothing that is static and not changing.

That is why I need you to engage your imagination for a moment and try to see things from God's perspective. I call this the *God's eye view*. God is the Creator of time. That means that time has no hold on Him since it is an element of His creation. As an element of His creation, it is impossible for the Creator to be bound by His own creation.

If time is God's creation, then He has access to past, present, and future at once. He sees the end from the beginning. Not only can He see it, but He sees every decision and every choice you are going to make and its effect upon future generations.

As humans, we tend to only see our own lifetime. We really don't have much of a feel for what we are leaving behind and the power it has to change other generations. If we did, I think we would be more careful with our lives and our ideas so that we would not leave behind us a destructive force. We must understand that God's dealings with us are with a view far beyond our vapor of life. Yes, we have a lifespan that is composed of a certain number of days, but the effect of my life can go well beyond my life on earth. Therefore, God deals with us as it concerns the whole of the future and the impact that our life can have upon it.

As you make the imaginative leap out of time and look at God's movements from a timeless perspective, you will be able to see the strategies of God in the making; not necessarily future strategies, but past ones. These grand designs might have remained unnoticed if we were not thinking from the perspective of timelessness.

What I am asking you to observe is a progression of government in the nation of Israel. You will find that it starts with man's form of government and progresses to God's form of government. Then, when we have found and identified God's form of government, we will look at it from a New Covenant perspective with the Church. Once this is done, we are then able to implement it into our own groups to the glory of God.

Israel did not start as a nation. Israel was a man. The nation of Israel has as its father, Abraham. Abraham was called out from the Chaldeans. God had invited him to leave his family and their idols. As Abraham progressed in faith, he also progressed in blessing and revelation.

Although Abraham had more than one child, only one of them was called the *son of promise*. Isaac was his name and he had two children; Essau, who he preferred, and Jacob. It was Jacob who wrestled with God and whose name was changed to Israel. One thing we see right away is that for some reason God uses the number twelve with regard to government.

Note that the son that Abraham sent away was also under the promise of God. What was the promise? *"I will make of you a multitude of people."* Ishmael had twelve sons. Jacob (Israel) had twelve sons that became the heads of twelve tribes. Jesus also had twelve apostles who would become the overseers of the Church. The pattern is there; however, they are only a family at this point. Families have as their government a father and a mother. When the family of Jacob entered Egypt there were seventy of them. They were eventually enslaved. When Moses is sent to free them, it is four hundred years later. They had already established heads of the different tribes. This is where we pick up God's movement among this special people.

Moses

We are going to start our journey with Moses. Moses, from the perspective of the five fold ministry, was a prophet and an apostle. Moses is called a prophet in the Bible so his being a prophet is never in question. That raises the question, *"How do we know that Moses fit the description of an apostle as well?"* In order to answer this we have to look at what an apostle does. Apostles are sent ones. Was Moses sent by God? Apostles are congregation builders. Was Moses a builder of the congregation? Apostles bring structure to an organization. Did Moses bring structure to God's people, Israel? It may not be apparent now why this is important, but you will see soon why it is. For the sake of argument, let us consider Moses, the apostle/prophet leader God has placed to lead a people.

As a prophet, Moses was different than the other prophets. We find this in Numbers 12:6-8 where God says, *"if there is a prophet in the land, I will speak to them in a dream or vision. But not so with My servant Moses. With Him, I will speak face to face."* After that, Moses predicts concerning Jesus when he said that God was going to, *"send another prophet like me. Him you should listen to,"* (Deuteronomy 18:15, Acts 3:19-22) What this means is that from the time of Moses to the time of Jesus, there were no prophets to whom God would speak face to face.

I think we could also argue that Moses was a shepherd, a teacher, and an evangelist. In demonstrating these offices of ministry, he was the ultimate type and shadow of Jesus. Just for a point of reference, I do not ascribe to the idea that today people can hold all five offices of ministry. We know that Apostle Paul held the office of teacher and apostle. This concept that a single individual is all five callings has no biblical basis from what I have found.

For this chapter, however, I want to look at the apostle/prophet call upon Moses. We find in 1 Corinthians 12:28 a revelation that God appointed in the Church; first apostles, second prophets, and third teachers. This scripture is often quoted to show a hierarchical authority in the Church, but I believe it is a revelation of first in time, not first in authority. I also believe that this is a pattern that shows the necessity of the callings as it concerns building the Church.

I would also argue that Moses was called to be the High Priest rather than his brother, Aaron. Why do I think this? When Moses approached the burning bush and received the revelation of his call and destiny, he refused it in part. The part he refused was that of spokesperson. He argued with God that he was slow of speech and that he could not accomplish the call as God had defined it. God's response was that His anger burned against Moses. Consequently, God sent Aaron to be the spokesperson for Moses. I argue that if Moses would have believed that he whom God sends, God equips, Moses would have had the calling of High Priest and in this, would complete the picture of the Messiah!

Because Moses had these callings, he was the supreme leader over Israel. Remember, he is a picture of the Christ to come. **Moses shadowed for us Christ, the Head of the Church.** It is also interesting to discover how Moses led Israel. He did so by never making a decision for himself. He always inquired of God. This is also a powerful picture of Jesus Who said, *"I do nothing except what I see my Father doing."* However, this way of governance by man was not God's chosen method to govern His people. Moses was simply shadow typing the Christ to come.

If we look back in time even before Moses, the government of the nation Israel started under a patriarchal style of governance. That is, Israel started out as a family and in the family, the patriarchs ruled. When Israel went to Egypt they were not a nation, they were still a family since they numbered only seventy people. It was during the four-hundred years in Egypt that Israel grew from a family to a community and finally into a nation.

The patriarchal rule would not work for a nation because of the vast number of people to lead. As a result, each tribe had elected elders to be their leaders. This is collegiate rule or rule by council. Moses, a type of Messiah, was sent to whom? He was sent to the elders of Israel (Exodus 3:16). This is important in order to demonstrate that Moses is being a type of Messiah, revealing to us what the government of the Church was going to look like.

Remember, God is outside of time and space and is watching Israel progress into the people of God. Everything Moses said to do, the nation did. This shows us that all the people were submitted to the authority of Moses, save a few who rebelled. Moses was, by position, the head of Israel. Keep in mind, this is not God's desired form of governance in that Moses is a man, but it is a picture of the type of government if one looks at Moses as a type of Christ. Nevertheless, this form of government was the necessity of the moment as it concerned Israel.

Next, in regard to the governance of God, He commanded Moses to bring the entire congregation to the mountain where He would speak to them as He had been doing with Moses on the mountain. God wanted to speak to the people the very thing He had already revealed to Moses on the mountain. Why? I believe it is because God wanted to be in relationship with them as the Husband of Israel. The words Moses received on the mountain were the words of the covenant. God wanted to enter into covenant with His people. God did not want to have a single *set man* rule over Israel who would stand between them and Him. God wanted to rule over Israel.

Truth be told, the congregation was not receptive and as a result, God had to deal with them through Moses. I want you to ponder this for a moment. It reminds me of a father who has gone into the military while his children are only two or three years old. Then upon returning two years later and looking forward to seeing his children, they are frightened by his voice and run from him in fear. What that must do to hurt a father's heart. This is what happened to God. Israel suffered from the same problem that children suffer from that react in fear when they come face to face with their father. They are not mature. Immaturity causes people to misjudge things and it caused Israel to misjudge their meeting with God.

Israel told Moses on that day that they wanted him to hear from God and they would do everything God said by his mouth to do. This meant that if anyone wanted to inquire of the Lord, they would have to ask Moses and he would petition God for them. God did not want it to be this way. He wanted them to feel safe enough to come to Him directly. God wanted them to trust Him enough to come to Him openly. Because they were not willing, by necessity, Moses became the set man over the congregation. We must remember that we are witnessing the birth of a nation and a way of governance being implemented.

One of the problems of a single man rule is that everyone looks to that man. Concerning the Church, this is precisely the dilemma. Too many people are looking to the man in the Church, and not the God over the Church. However, when a council rules, the people seem to look past the council to the One Who is the King. If it is true that God did not want a single man to rule, then we should begin to see a transition in the next leadership structure when Moses passes from the earth.

Numbers 27:16-21 NKJV

Verses 16-17"Let the Lord, the God of the spirits of all flesh, set a man over the congregation, who may go out before them and go in before them, who may lead them out and bring them in, that the congregation of the Lord may not be like sheep which have no shepherd."

Moses' desire was to continue the same type of rule. Moses did not have God's mind concerning the governance of His people. He wanted to continue the status quo. This way of governance had become comfortable to him. God, though, was about to make a slight transition to begin to mold the nation of Israel's paradigm to accept His form of governance.

Verses 18-19 And the Lord said to Moses: "Take Joshua the son of Nun with you, a man in whom is the Spirit, and lay your hand on him; set him before Eleazar the priest and before all the congregation, and inaugurate him in their sight."

The necessity for another leader was based in the needs of the people. Since the people had rejected the idea that they were to hear from God, they required a person who would hear from Him for them. In this example I see the same thing happening in the Church today. Many people will travel from seminar to seminar to hear from this prophet or that prophet or they will seek audience with the pastor just as Israel would do with Moses when God wants them to come to Him, to inquire of Him, and to build a relationship with Him.

What would have happened if the congregation of Israel desired to have a relationship with God in the same manner as Moses? This would have changed the dynamic of the government structure. The same goes for the Church. If the people begin to build that type of relationship with God it will have the effect of creating the atmosphere where the government structure of the Church can change.

It is obvious by Moses' response that he is worried about the congregation. After all, Moses is the only one that has been hearing from God with regard to leading Israel. Now what if Moses had coequals ruling with him? Would he have been worried about the congregation in his absence? A council of leaders hearing from God would have relieved the worry that Moses had simply because others would already be in place to rule the nation of Israel at his passing.

Suffice it to say, however, many leaders use this verse to claim their hierarchical authority as the preferred governance of God. They say that the apostle is the set man and use this scripture to forward that idea. Nevertheless, note what happens through generational timelines. If the set man rule is not God's preference with regard to human governance, then we should see a transition take place that shows us God is weaning Israel off of this type of rule.

> **Verse 20** *And you shall give **some** of your authority to him, that all the congregation of the children of Israel may be obedient.*

Pay attention to the use of the word "some." *(Note: the word "some" is not in the original Hebrew; however, if you look at the Hebrew word used for authority it denotes a portion of authority so in this case the word "some" is correct in bringing clarity to the text.)* This is the first indication that a change in the structure of authority is going to take place. Moses could not give Joshua the totality of his mantle. That mantle of authority is now being split. Some of the authority would be given to Joshua and some would be given to another.

> **Verse 21** *"He shall stand before Eleazar the priest, who shall inquire before the Lord for him by the judgment of the Urim. At his word they shall go out, and at his word they shall come in, he and all the children of Israel with him—all the congregation."*

Notice how and in what way God is dividing the authority. The mantle (apostolic and prophetic authority) of Moses is being divided. The apostolic authority was to rest upon Joshua, whereas the prophetic authority was to rest upon Eleazar. God is now weaning the people off their need to have a single leader. Joshua was to be one type of leader, whereas Eleazar was to hear from God and instruct Joshua as to what God wanted him to do and in that Eleazar became a different type of leader.

Joshua

Observe that neither Joshua nor Eleazar could complete the job without submitting to one another's position and gifting. Joshua had the people's ear, but he could not hear from God like Eleazar. Eleazar could hear from God, but did not have the people's ear. Eleazar needed Joshua to get the message of God to the people and Joshua needed Eleazar to get the message from God. In this arrangement, we see the first picture of God's desired governance and the birth of the five fold ministry.

This is often the case in the local church today. The people will give their ear to listen to the apostle, but not necessarily the prophet. Hence, the apostle needs the prophet to get the vision and direction of God. The prophet can get that vision and direction, but they cannot always communicate it to the people and get them to hear and act upon it like the apostle can. This sets up the team mentality of the council. This is what God desires in order that people would see Him as their King, rather than looking to a set man. The prophet is tasked to hear, whereas the apostle is tasked to communicate and build. **Nevertheless, this is still not a complete picture of what God had in mind for the governing of His people.**

The nagging question then will be, *"Is there another transition of downgrading hierarchy at the passing of Joshua?"* Before we go to this period in time through which I want you to take that step outside of time and space and see the wisdom of God, I want you to consider yourself. God does not look at your life in the context of your lifespan. He is dealing with you based upon the effect that your life is going to have from this point in time on into the future, even after you are long gone.

What are your great-great-great-grandchildren going to receive from you? What is the world going to receive from you generations from now? You have the power to bring them blessing or cursing by how you live your life today. Your life does not just impact yourself, but those around you today, as well as generations to come. The question that follows is, *"What do you want to leave in front of you?"* Do you want to leave a pattern of addiction, sexual immorality, cursing, etc., or do you want to leave a pattern of peace, love, righteousness, and other positive attributes?

In the leading of God's Church, processes have been performed certain ways for a long time. Many of these "ways" are not what God designed for His Church. However, because governance has looked the same for such a long time, change will most likely only bring whining, complaining, speculating, and even anger. The response is often, *"We have been doing it this way for hundreds of years, so why change?"*

Because of this response, change is often averted, not attempted at all, or slow in coming. What we need to understand as leaders is that we will have to give an account for our leadership. We should be careful and willing to come into agreement with the Spirit in leading His Church, or we risk the loss of His presence in the Church.

When Israel rebelled, there came a time where God refused to go before them. Instead of God going before them in the cloud by day and the fire by night, He sent the angel of the Lord to do so. This is a provoking reminder that God's presence in His congregation is conditioned on the willingness of that congregation and leadership to follow His leading and direction as well as every command of instruction.

For a moment, I would like to back up in time a bit and reveal God the Great Strategist. Because He is the Great Strategist, you need to understand that the things He gives you to do today may be for a people that are not even in existence yet. We can see this in God's dealing with the nation of Israel. Before God began to shift to a style of government that is marked by a rule by council, He had to create the framework of His preference of governance beforehand. Doing so would assure that it would be in place generations later when He makes the shift from the set man to the council. I think this is just an amazing view of God's transcendence of time.

> **Deuteronomy 16:18** *"You shall appoint for yourself judges and officers in all your towns which the Lord your God is giving you, according to your tribes, and they shall judge the people with righteous judgment."*

Moses is still ruling as the set man at this time. Yet, we see God is establishing a framework for His type of government so that it will be in place when He finally weans the congregation off of the set man style of rule. As I looked at this, in prayer I asked God why He was against the set man type of rule. It was at this moment that the Spirit of God came crashing into my consciousness and He said, *"It is because I love them."* This will begin to make more sense as we proceed.

> **Deuteronomy 17:8-13 ~NKJV~** *If a matter arises which is too hard for you to judge, between degrees of guilt for bloodshed, between one judgment or another, or between one punishment or another, matters of controversy within your gates, then you shall arise and go up to the place which the Lord your God chooses.*
>
> *9 And you shall come to the priests, the Levites, and to the judge there in those days, and inquire of them; they shall pronounce upon you the sentence of judgment.*

10 You shall do according to the sentence which they pronounce upon you in that place which the Lord chooses. And you shall be careful to do according to all that they order you.

11 According to the sentence of the law in which they instruct you, according to the judgment which they tell you, you shall do; you shall not turn aside to the right hand or to the left from the sentence which they pronounce upon you.

12 Now the man who acts presumptuously and will not heed the priest who stands to minister there before the Lord your God, or the judge, that man shall die. So you shall put away the evil from Israel.

13 And all the people shall hear and fear, and no longer act presumptuously.

Remember, this statement was given during the rule of Moses. God is shifting the paradigm of the nation of Israel to achieve the rule by council which would allow God to be their King. God was establishing the authority of the judge and the priest. There is also the warning not to act presumptuously to the rule of the priest or judge. To act presumptuously is to anticipate based upon my wants and desires or beliefs.

If we were to fast forward to twenty-first century thought concerning the Church, an example of acting presumptuously would be to consider my discipleship as a series of encounters with men and women of God rather than a submission to a local body and its leadership. You might think you know better, but God has stated through His Word and His ministers what discipleship is and the necessity of it.

This seems to be the norm today rather than the exception in the current culture of Christianity. If there is to be a destiny fulfilled, it must be done in the order God designed. Otherwise, our actions tell a story of rebellion and disbelief in the authority of God to identify and call us to our specific destinies.

If we slough off God's way of achieving it, thinking that it is too difficult or not culturally correct, we will not attain what God created us to attain. Each of us carries the burden of God for our particular destiny. God's purpose for us will not be realized if we do not carry that burden by following His leading and His instructions.

How many times have people left discipleship by presuming that they were ready to enter into their ministry? Apostle Paul, one of the greatest minds of the New Testament, having three PhD's, submitted to discipleship. He became a teacher in the church at Antioch and at the Spirit's leading, he was sent out to begin his ministry. Are you going to carry your ministry training to the end, or will you bail out because you think you are anointed, gifted, and charismatic enough to do so? You will be responsible for how you answer this question for yourself.

Transition

> **Joshua 23:2** *that Joshua called for all Israel, for their elders and their heads and their judges and their officers, and said to them, "I am old, advanced in years."*

Notice that whereas Moses called Joshua and Eleazar, Joshua called for the elders, heads, judges, and officers. This is another shift toward the government of God. Note that elders had heads and judges had officers. These were no doubt associates that helped in the accomplishment of the duties of the elders and judges.

> **Joshua 24:1** *Then Joshua gathered all the tribes of Israel to Shechem, and called for the elders of Israel and for their heads and their judges and their officers; and they presented themselves before God.*

Now that they are assembled, note that they are assembled not just before Joshua, but also before God. Joshua was now going to give them instructions, not to one man, not even to two men, but to a whole council.

> **Joshua 24:14-15** *"Now, therefore, fear the Lord and serve Him in sincerity and truth; and put away the gods which your fathers served beyond the River and in Egypt, and serve the Lord. If it is disagreeable in your sight to serve the Lord, choose for yourselves today whom you will serve: whether the gods which your fathers served which were beyond the River, or the gods of the Amorites in whose land you are living; but as for me and my house, we will serve the Lord."*

Joshua is presenting the ultimate decision for any leader. Will you serve the Lord? Will you serve God, or are you going to serve self? Will you serve God or do you have your eyes on that position of leadership? Will you serve the Lord, or will you serve to enrich yourself? These are the crucial questions that every leader must ask of themselves and come to terms with. The reason this is so important is that the authority has now gone from one set man, Moses, to two set men, Joshua and Eleazar, and finally to the council of elders and judges. Each one will preside over their respective areas.

Joshua 24:21-27

Verses 21-22 The people said to Joshua, "No, but we will serve the Lord." Joshua said to the people, "You are witnesses against yourselves that you have chosen for yourselves the Lord, to serve Him." And they said, "We are witnesses."

Joshua was reminding the leaders that their confession was not just before men, but they had assembled before God. They claimed that they would serve the Lord. They talked a good talk, but were they actually walking and living that way? This is a reminder that all of us can make good confessions, but what we are actually doing reveals the truth about us. Are we living the confession, or is it more profession than possession?

Verses 23-24 "Now therefore, put away the foreign gods which are in your midst, and incline your hearts to the Lord, the God of Israel." The people said to Joshua, "We will serve the Lord our God and we will obey His voice."

Here was the answer. They were still serving false gods. They still had idols in their houses. They were claiming to serve the real God, but in action they were committing spiritual adultery. Here they are making a confession when they have not made the move to actually do it. This had to ring very hallow in Joshua's ears.

Verses 25-27 So Joshua made a covenant with the people that day, and made for them a statute and an ordinance in Shechem. And Joshua wrote these words in the book of the law of God; and he took a large stone and set it up there under the oak that was by the sanctuary of the Lord. Joshua said to all

*the people, "Behold, this stone shall be for a
witness against us, for it has heard all the words of
the Lord which He spoke to us; thus it shall be for a
witness against you, so that you do not deny your
God."*

The Hebrew word for "covenant" is "cutting." It is a picture of a couple of things. First, there is blood spilled. To cut a covenant they would take a series of animals and slay them. Next, they would cut them in half and separate the halves to make a pathway between the parts. Then each person that was entering into covenant would pass between the carcasses and this would be a way of saying that if I break with this covenant, I forfeit my life.

The second picture to cutting is the inscription of the covenant. To Moses was given the covenant etched in rock and now here at the end of Joshua's life, he did the same thing. The rock not only heard, but also inscribed upon it were the words of the Lord that He spoke to them. It was to be a witness. What other stone is called a witness?

> ***Deuteronomy 31:26*** *"Take this book of the law and
> place it beside the ark of the covenant of the Lord
> your God, that it may remain there as a **witness**
> against you."*

> ***Exodus 25:21-22*** *"You shall put the mercy seat on
> top of the ark, and in the ark you shall put the
> **testimony** which I will give to you. There I will meet
> with you; and from above the mercy seat, from
> between the two cherubim which are upon the ark
> of the **testimony**, I will speak to you about all that I
> will give you in commandment for the sons of
> Israel."*

The Hebrew word for "witness" is the root word for "testimony." "Covenant," "testimony," and "witness" are grouped together. That means that where there is a covenant there is also a witness and a testimony. That witness and testimony are the words written upon the covenant.

> **Acts 1:8** *"but you will receive power when the Holy Spirit has come upon you; and you shall be My **witnesses** both in Jerusalem, and in all Judea and Samaria, and even to the remotest part of the earth."*

When God cut a covenant with us, we became His witnesses because He has written His laws upon our hearts and minds.

> **Hebrews 10:16-18** *"This is the covenant that I will make with them after those days, says the Lord: I will put My laws upon their heart, And on their mind I will write them, He then says, And their sins and their lawless deeds I will remember no more. Now where there is forgiveness of these things, there is no longer any offering for sin."*

Where were the stones of testimony located? They were in the Ark of Covenant. What is on top of that ark? It is the mercy seat. What is the mercy seat? It is the throne of God. When you become a believer in Jesus, God writes His laws upon your heart and mind and declares that you will become His witnesses. This means that you are now His ark of testimony and He dwells in you and your heart has become His throne. **You are now a living testimony, a living witness, and a living stone!**

> **1 Peter 2:4-5** *And coming to Him as to a living stone which has been rejected by men, but is choice*

*and precious in the sight of God, you also, **as living stones**, are being built up as a spiritual house for a holy priesthood, to offer up spiritual sacrifices acceptable to God through Jesus Christ.*

Gideon

Now we enter into the period of the judges. God has weaned the people of Israel off having a set man over them. Councils of judges and elders now rule them with God as their King. We open this section with Gideon who is a judge. Gideon had just been granted a great victory with an army of only three hundred men. Upon returning, the people rejoiced and asked of Gideon a very telling question.

> *Judges 8:22-23 Then the men of Israel said to Gideon, **"Rule over us, both you and your son, also your son's son**, for you have delivered us from the hand of Midian." But Gideon said to them, "I will not rule over you, nor shall my son rule over you; **the Lord shall rule over you."***

By the time we get to the judge Gideon, it is already understood by the people that God is to be King while His council is to rule on earth over Israel. We know this based upon Gideon's response to the people who asked him to rule over them as a king. Why is it that people always want a man to rule over them? They want a man who has like lusts and passions and who is completely imperfect and unable to make accurate decisions to rule over them. Here we have the most benevolent Being in the universe ruling over the nation and they want to downgrade.

Even though Gideon answered correctly to the request to rule over them, he did overstep his position and instituted a tax that only the King had power to do. Because Gideon took a position that he did not have and instituted a tax on his behalf, the result of this tax became Gideon's undoing.

> *Judges 8:24-27 Yet Gideon said to them, "I would request of you, that each of you give me an earring from his spoil." (For they had gold earrings, because they were Ishmaelites.)*
>
> *25 They said, "We will surely give them." So they spread out a garment, and every one of them threw an earring there from his spoil.*
>
> *26 The weight of the gold earrings that he requested was 1,700 shekels of gold, besides the crescent ornaments and the pendants and the purple robes which were on the kings of Midian, and besides the neck bands that were on their camels' necks.*
>
> *27 Gideon made it into an ephod, and placed it in his city, Ophrah, and all Israel played the harlot with it there, so that it became a snare to Gideon and his household.*

The gold that Gideon took in that taxation became a trap. Anytime we go beyond our authority and take from God His authority we ensnare ourselves and our households. Again, our actions can affect generations to come. Gideon's whole house was taken into idolatry because of this.

Abimelekh

Now we advance again to the next generation. Gideon has died and he left behind seventy sons; one of which was a scoundrel. Abimelekh was his name. Note also that Abimelekh was born of a harlot whose nationality was not of the nation of Israel.

Abimelekh's name is interesting because in that culture, names were given according to what was going on in the parents' lives or something in relation to the birth. Abimelekh in Hebrew is a compound word. Abba means father and Melekh means king. In other words "My father is king." This gives insight into Gideon's heart. Gideon apparently started to see himself as their king. He just could not get that moment out of his head when the people asked him to be their king. No doubt, he would lay awake at night pondering that special day. Then it began to take hold of his life and even though earlier he had the correct response, now the pride of life is beginning to get a grip on him.

This also must have had a profound effect upon his son Abimelekh's life. After all, if his father is the king then he must be a prince in line to the throne. Because of this, Abimelekh had thoughts of grandeur. He was the son of a harlot so he went to his mother's people and presented himself as a king. Because Gideon had seventy sons that were all born of Israelite mothers except for Abimelekh, he shrewdly appealed to his own people on the basis that they would not want an Israelite ruling over them. The reason, of course, was that Israelite rulers would give preference to their own people. An Israelite would not have the people of Abimelekh's best interest at heart. Because of his convincing argument, they accepted him as king.

Once Abimelekh is anointed as king, he gathers a band of men and proceeds to wipe out any heir to his throne. In his attempt to kill them all, one of his brothers escaped. The one that escaped fled to an overhang where he could be heard by all the people.

Judges 9:8-13 *"Once the trees went forth to anoint a king over them, and they said to the olive tree, 'Reign over us!'*

9 But the olive tree said to them, 'Shall I leave my fatness with which God and men are honored, and go to wave over the trees?'

10 Then the trees said to the fig tree, 'You come, reign over us!'

11 But the fig tree said to them, 'Shall I leave my sweetness and my good fruit, and go to wave over the trees?'

12 Then the trees said to the vine, 'You come, reign over us!'

13 But the vine said to them, 'Shall I leave my new wine, which cheers God and men, and go to wave over the trees?'"

The point being made is that God's people are too busy being who they are called to be and bearing fruit at it, that they have no need or desire to be a king. True leaders are not position seekers; they are busy bearing fruit by leading. The fruit a true leader seeks is to bring their followers to the place where they are leading them; that the people become leaders in their fields. This is the picture being painted here. True leaders are too busy leading to be tempted by position.

> *Judges 9:14-15 "Finally all the trees said to the bramble, 'You come, reign over us!' The bramble said to the trees, 'If in truth you are anointing me as king over you, come and take refuge in my shade; but if not, may fire come out from the bramble and consume the cedars of Lebanon.'"*

On the other hand, those that aspire to the position of king or head are the bramble. They are so consumed with the delusion of power that they will do anything to ascend to a throne. Those that seek position are the ones that you do not want to lead. They are the most dangerous and will abuse the position and those they lead. I am not speaking of our own political process in America. The system that we have forces people to *run for office.* What we must do in this system is to look at the motive of running for office to discern between those who want it for the position and those who want to lead people to a better place morally and financially.

Transition From Samuel to Saul

Now that Israel has been under the government of God during the period of the judges for quite some time, there is no doubt who their King is. Still, the people want change. Their reason for change is for the nation of Israel to be like the other nations.

I see the Church doing this same thing today. I have heard many times that the Church needs to be set up like a business and it needs to be structured like secular organizations. This is just an appeal to do things the same way as the world. It may even make perfect sense from the standpoint of logic. On the other hand, God does not do things the way the world does. His ways transcend human wisdom and understanding.

> *1 Samuel 8:1-5 And it came about when Samuel was old that he appointed his sons judges over Israel. Now the name of his firstborn was Joel, and the name of his second, Abijah; they were judging in Beersheba. His sons, however, did not walk in his ways, but turned aside after dishonest gain and took bribes and perverted justice. Then all the elders of Israel gathered together and came to Samuel at Ramah; and they said to him, "Behold, you have*

grown old, and your sons do not walk in your ways.
Now appoint a king for us to judge us like all the
nations."

Who was it that came to Samuel? It was the council of
elders. They desired to have a king. God was now being rejected as
King of Israel. It took three generations to bring the people to the
place where they were comfortable having God as their King, and
in one fleeting moment, they plunge themselves back under the
rule of a mere man. Now it is going to make more sense as to why
when I prayed and asked God, *"Why are you against us having a
set man?"* that His response was, *"Because I love you."*

> *1 Samuel 8:6-9 But the thing was displeasing in the
> sight of Samuel when they said, "Give us a king to
> judge us." And Samuel prayed to the Lord. The
> Lord said to Samuel, "Listen to the voice of the
> people in regard to all that they say to you, for they
> have not rejected you, but they have rejected Me
> from being king over them.* **"Like all the deeds
> which they have done since the day that I brought
> them up from Egypt even to this day—in that they
> have forsaken Me and served other gods—so they
> are doing to you also.** *"Now then, listen to their
> voice; however, you shall solemnly warn them and
> tell them of the procedure of the king who will reign
> over them."*

God likens asking for a king to serving other gods. How is
it then that we have churches structured in a way that causes them
to commit this same idolatry? If we, as a Church, are to have
God's presence in the Church, we are going to have to structure
ourselves the way God wants us structured. It has been the pattern
of God that when men reject Him from ruling over them, that He

leaves. He will not violate their freedom of choice, but He will judge it.

1 Samuel 8:10-22 So Samuel spoke all the words of the Lord to the people who had asked of him a king. He said, "This will be the procedure of the king who will reign over you: he will take your sons and place them for himself in his chariots and among his horsemen and they will run before his chariots. He will appoint for himself commanders of thousands and of fifties, and some to do his plowing and to reap his harvest and to make his weapons of war and equipment for his chariots. He will also take your daughters for perfumers and cooks and bakers. He will take the best of your fields and your vineyards and your olive groves and give them to his servants."

*15 "He will take a tenth of your seed and of your vineyards and give to his officers and to his servants. He will also take your male servants and your female servants and your best young men and your donkeys and use them for his work. He will take a tenth of your flocks, and you yourselves will become his servants. Then you will cry out in that day because of your king **whom you have chosen for yourselves**, but the Lord will not answer you in that day."*

19 Nevertheless, the people refused to listen to the voice of Samuel, and they said, "No, but there shall be a king over us, that we also may be like all the nations, that our king may judge us and go out before us and fight our battles." Now after Samuel had heard all the words of the people, he repeated them in the Lord's hearing. The Lord said to Samuel, "Listen to their voice and appoint them a king." So Samuel said to the men of Israel, "Go every man to his city."

It may look as if God is not that bothered by this turn of events, but if we look in other places in Scripture we find the emotion of God is revealed at the time this took place and it was not at all pleasant. We could learn a lesson from this. When we are thrust upon the duties of leadership we need to allow God to have His place in our seat of authority.

> ***Hosea 13:10-11*** *Where now is your king That he may save you in all your cities, And your judges of whom you requested, "Give me a king and princes"?* **I gave you a king in My anger And took him away in My wrath.**

> ***Ezekiel 20:33-38*** *"As I live," declares the Lord God, "surely with a mighty hand and with an outstretched arm and with wrath poured out,* **I shall be king over you.** *I will bring you out from the peoples and gather you from the lands where you are scattered, with a mighty hand and with an outstretched arm and with wrath poured out; and I will bring you into the wilderness of the peoples, and there I will enter into judgment with you face to face."*

> *36 "As I entered into judgment with your fathers in the wilderness of the land of Egypt, so I will enter into judgment with you," declares the Lord God. "I will make you pass under the rod, and I will bring you into the bond of the covenant; and I will purge*

from you the rebels and those who transgress against Me; I will bring them out of the land where they sojourn, but they will not enter the land of Israel. Thus you will know that I am the Lord."

When we reject God as King, we are not only rejecting Him, but we are rejecting His kingdom as well. A kingdom is the domain of the king. It is the geographical sphere of authority and rule of a king. When we switch kings, we switch kingdoms. Only God is capable of ruling with the kind of beneficent authority that will place us in safety. If we switch kings, to what kingdom do we transfer ourselves?

> **Colossians 1:13** *For He rescued us from the domain of darkness, and transferred us to the kingdom of His beloved Son...*

> **John 8:12** *Then Jesus again spoke to them, saying, "I am the Light of the world; he who follows Me will not walk in the darkness, but will have the Light of life."*

> **John 18:33-37** *Therefore Pilate entered again into the Praetorium, and summoned Jesus and said to Him, "Are You the King of the Jews?" Jesus answered, "Are you saying this on your own initiative, or did others tell you about Me?" Pilate answered, "I am not a Jew, am I? Your own nation and the chief priests delivered You to me; what have You done?"*

> **36** *Jesus answered, "My kingdom is not of this world. If My kingdom were of this world, then My servants would be fighting so that I would not be handed over to the Jews; but as it is, My kingdom is*

not of this realm." Therefore Pilate said to Him,
*"So You are a king?" Jesus answered, **"You say***
correctly that I am a king. For this I have been
born, and for this I have come into the world, to
testify to the truth. Everyone who is of the truth
hears My voice."

If we are so foolish to think that we are running things ourselves we are deceived indeed. For when man chooses to usurp Christ's authority in His Church by setting himself up as the controlling head of the Church, that man is deceived and by deception has placed over himself the kingdom of darkness rather than the kingdom of light.

Future Kingdom

We have looked at the preferred government of God in the Old Testament and see that it was the period known as the judges. In this government, judges would judge and rule their respective areas, but the nation's Head or King was God. The ruling authority for that nation on earth was then the council of judges. There is more proof of this.

> ***1 Chronicles 17:6*** *"In all places where I have walked with all Israel, have I spoken a word with any of the **judges of Israel, whom I commanded to shepherd My people**, saying, 'Why have you not built for Me a house of cedar?' "*

When we move to the New Testament period, we find that Jesus has come to set in order His government over His people. He is to be their King. We see this evidenced in the way the Apostles carried out the governance of the Church after the departure of Jesus to sit upon His throne. Another proof of this type of government is found in the following Scripture.

Luke 19:11-27 While they were listening to these things, Jesus went on to tell a parable, because He was near Jerusalem, and they supposed that the kingdom of God was going to appear immediately. So He said, "A nobleman went to a distant country to receive a kingdom for himself, and then return. And he called ten of his slaves, and gave them ten minas and said to them, 'Do business with this until I come back.' **But his citizens hated him and sent a delegation after him, saying, 'We do not want this man to reign over us.'"**

"When he returned, after receiving the kingdom, he ordered that these slaves, to whom he had given the money, be called to him so that he might know what business they had done. The first appeared, saying, 'Master, your mina has made ten minas more.' And he said to him, 'Well done, good slave, because you have been faithful in a very little thing, you are to be in authority over ten cities.' The second came, saying, 'Your mina, master, has made five minas.' And he said to him also, 'And you are to be over five cities.' Another came, saying, 'Master, here is your mina, which I kept put away in a handkerchief; for I was afraid of you, because you are an exacting man; you take up what you did not lay down and reap what you did not sow.'"

"He said to him, 'By your own words I will judge you, you worthless slave. Did you know that I am an exacting man, taking up what I did not lay down and reaping what I did not sow? Then why did you not put my money in the bank, and having come, I would have collected it with interest?' Then he said

to the bystanders, 'Take the mina away from him
and give it to the one who has the ten minas.' And
they said to him, 'Master, he has ten minas
already.' I tell you that to everyone who has, more
shall be given, but from the one who does not have,
even what he does have shall be taken away. ***But***
these enemies of mine, who did not want me to
reign over them, bring them here and slay them in
my presence."

A couple things should be noted here. First in this parable, there was a group of people that did not want to be ruled by God. At the end of this parable, these rebels were slain in the presence of the King. The other thing that should be noted is that the ruling of the kingdom was in the hands of a council or group of people, not a single individual. This is just another proof of God's preferred governance.

We have yet to look at the future kingdom to see if we can get another piece of evidence for the preferred government of God. The greatest picture into this future kingdom is when Jesus told His disciples their future.

Matthew 19:28 And Jesus said to them, "Truly I say
to you, that you who have followed Me, in the
regeneration when the Son of Man will sit on His
glorious throne, you also shall sit upon twelve
thrones, ***judging the twelve tribes of Israel".***

The picture is clear. Jesus will sit upon His glorious throne to rule the earth and the twelve will rule over the nation of Israel with Jesus as Head over them. Notice the term *judging*. What was God's preferred governance in the Old Testament period? It was the period of the judges. God will reestablish His government through the rule and reign of Jesus. This is why Isaiah says of the

Messiah, *"The government shall be upon His shoulders."* We can either come into agreement with God in the ruling of Jesus over His Church or we can rule the Church ourselves as a set man out of rebellion and suffer the result.

If we are to have the presence of God corporately we need to be structured in a way that allows for Jesus to be the Head of His Church. The pattern we have during the period of the judges is that God would rule through His judges by council. This is not to dismiss that there were judges who ruled singularly over a region, yet we see councils in the form of elders being a part of that rule.

What would church government look like if it is to pattern the period of the judges? For that answer we move to the next chapter.

Church Government

Chapter Two

In this chapter we will look at the *Church;* we will define it and we will look at how it is defined by today's Christian religious culture. We will also look at church government; define it; look at how it is defined by today's standard. In the end, I hope to show the gap that exists between what the Bible has defined and what man has constructed. The purpose of this is to get us back to the biblical application of governing the Church so that we can have the corporate presence of God.

The Church

When I survey the current landscape in regard to the Church, I have to wonder what has taken place in church government that has had the effect of removing us so far from the structure that was established by the early church fathers. Even the word *church* has been so corrupted that the world thinks of a building when defining the term.

If we just keep to what the Bible has defined for us in regard to church structure, we can bring growth and power back to the Body of Christ. This is not a condemnation of men, but a criticism of the enemy's tactic to neutralize the power the Church has the potential of wielding. Having said that, we start this chapter by taking a look at how today's society defines the word *church.*

DEFINITION – CHURCH

Language – English

CHURCH[Middle English chirche, from Old English cirice, ultimately from Late Greek

*kyriakon, from Greek, neuter of kyriakos of the
lord, from kyrios lord, master; akin to Sanskrit
Œuµra hero, warrior]*

(before 12th century)

*1 : a building for public and especially Christian
worship 2 : the clergy or officialdom of a
religious body 3 : a body or organization of
religious believers: as a : the whole Body of
Christians b : denomination c : congregation 4 :
a public divine worship ágoes to Church every
Sundayñ 5 : the clerical profession áconsidered
the Church as a possible careerñ [1]*

We have a problem already. This English word "church" is
derived from the Greek adjective *kyrialos* as used in such phrases
as *kyriakon doma,* meaning *the Lord's house,* which is a Christian
place of worship. Nevertheless, the biblical interpretation of the
word "church" comes from a different Greek word source.

DEFINITION – CHURCH

Language – Greek

1577 ekklesia ek-klay-see'-ah

*1) a gathering of citizens called out from their
homes into some public place, an assembly 1a) an
assembly of the people convened at the public
place of the council for the purpose of
deliberating 1d3) those who anywhere, in a city,*

---

[1] *(Mirriam-Webster, Incorporated, 1993)*

village, constitute such a company and are united into one body [2]

Therefore, on the one hand we see that, by men, church is defined as a building, but biblically it is described as a people. There is a stark and drastic contrast between a church building and an assemblage of people. If the biblical church is an assembly of people, we need to find out what constitutes an assembly.

DEFINITION – ASSEMBLY

Language – English

as•sem•bly -åsem-ble\ noun

1: a company of persons gathered for deliberation and legislation, worship, or entertainment [3]

The question then is, *"How many souls does it take to make an assembly?"* Why is this an important question to answer? It is important because if the church is defined as an assembly, then we need to know how many people it would take to make a church so that we can define what constitutes an official church from a biblical perspective. Hopefully, this will have the effect of removing mindsets and paradigms in regard to what is considered a church and what is not.

It would seem logical that an assembly is a gathering of two or more people. If this is so, then we need to have a minimum of two souls to create what is, in the eyes of God, called a church. Will this definition stand up to the scrutiny of Scripture?

---

[2] *(Logos Research Systems, Inc, 1995)*

[3] *(Mirriam-Webster, Incorporated, 1993)*

Matthew 18:20 *"For where two or three have gathered together in My name, there I am in their midst."*

Jesus identifies what would constitute an official assembly. It is the gathering of **two or three souls** in His name. When this is accomplished, He sanctions that meeting with His presence. One could not ask for a greater endorsement of a meeting than to have the Lord present there. Biblically, we see both small and large gatherings that are called a church. Why is it that small assemblies of two or three persons are not considered a valid church by bigger assemblies? For someone to scoff at a home church, for instance, would be biblically unacceptable if we define *church* in the same manner that Jesus had.

1 Corinthians 16:19 *The churches of Asia greet you. Aquila and Prisca greet you heartily in the Lord, with the **church that is in their house**.*

We see the example of a large gathering in the book of Acts where 5,000 souls were added to the assembly through one sermon given by Peter. So right from the start we have a sanctioning of the smallest church (two or three) and we have the sanctioning of a large church. We must also make the distinction between the local church and the universal Church.

- ✓ The local church is an assembly that is located in different geographical areas. For instance, Paul refers to the church which is at Ephesus. This is the local church.

- ✓ The universal Church is the conglomeration of all believers from biblical times until now as well as those believers yet to come. It is all inclusive of every believer saved during the Church age.

✓ The *living* universal Church includes those individuals who are Christians and are alive today. It does not matter to what group or organization they belong; what matters is their belief in Christ.

We cannot identify someone as a Christian simply because he goes to a certain organized religion on a certain day of the week. In almost every Christian organization there are those who are part of the Body of Christ, or the Church, and there are those who are not. Affiliation with a particular religion does not and cannot save anyone! It takes belief from the heart in Jesus as personal Savior and public confession of Him to be a member of Christ's Church, not affiliation with an organization.

Church Structure

What we see today as church government is mostly a hierarchical system when, as best as I can gather, the early church government was collegiate. What I mean by *hierarchical* is a body of presbytery organized into successive ranks or grades with each level being subordinate to the authority of the one above with a head pastor at the top. Is this really what Jesus had in mind for His Church?

What I mean by *collegiate* is a body of presbytery having a common purpose or shared duties: e.g. a college of surgeons. Our physical bodies are a college of members; the Body of Christ is a college of members. The etymology of the word "college" is a compound Latin word that means "to join" and "authorized representative." So what we really need for church structure is a council of authorized representatives; each submitting to the gifts and callings of all other council members. St. Clement, one of the early church fathers, said it better than I can:

"QUOTE"

*Clement of Rome, Chapter 38 - Let our whole body, then, be preserved in, Christ Jesus; and **let every one be subject to his neighbor, according to the special gift bestowed upon him**. Let the strong not despise the weak, and let the weak show respect unto the strong. Let the rich man provide for the wants of the poor; and let the poor man bless God, because He hath given him one by whom his need may be supplied.*

Let the wise man display his wisdom, not by [mere] words, but through good deeds. Let the humble not bear testimony to himself, but leave witness to be borne to him by another. Let him that is pure in the flesh not grow proud of it, and boast, knowing that it was another who bestowed on him the gift of continence.

Let us consider, then, brethren, of what matter we were made,--who and what manner of beings we came into the world, as it were out of a sepulcher, and from utter darkness. He who made us and fashioned us, having prepared His bountiful gifts for us before we were born, introduced us into His world. Since, therefore, we receive all these things from Him, we ought for everything to give Him thanks; to whom be glory for ever and ever. Amen. [4]

---

[4] *--St. Clement (Schaff)*

Although Clement's words are inclusive of the whole Body of Christ, it is also relevant to the leadership who belong to that same Body. What we see in our churches today is primarily a system of hierarchy. Is this what Jesus set forth for us in regard to church government? Since we are identified as the Body of Christ, we need to look at the Church like a real human body. This analogy is set forth in a number of verses. If it is true that we are all collected as one body then who is the head of this body? Who gives the direction and commands which bring fluidity, movement, and purpose to the body?

> *Ephesians 4:15-16 But speaking the truth in love, we are to grow up in all aspects into Him, **who is the head, even Christ**, from whom the whole body, being fitted and held together by that which every joint supplies, according to the proper working of each individual part, causes the growth of the body for the building up of itself in love.*

This discussion causes us to face another issue we see that is common among us. What about denominations? Is this a biblical principle established by God? Is it the will of God that believers divide into groups according to doctrinal differences?

> *1 Corinthians 1:10-13 Now I exhort you, brethren, by the name of our Lord Jesus Christ, that you all agree, and there be no divisions among you, but you be made complete in the same mind and in the same judgment. For I have been informed concerning you, my brethren, by Chloe's people, that there are quarrels among you. Now I mean this, that each one of you is saying, "I am of Paul," and "I of Apollos," and "I of Cephas," and "I of Christ." Has Christ been divided? Paul was not crucified for*

you, was he? Or were you baptized in the name of Paul?

The Apostle Paul is dealing with the local church that is in Corinth with regard to division. They are beginning to divide along denominational lines based on personalities or perhaps even doctrinal differences or nuances associated with each person named. One group is claiming to hold to the teachings of Paul; another is holding to the teachings of Apollos; another is holding to the teachings of Cephas (Peter); and another is holding to the teachings of Christ.

It needs to be noted that doctrinal differences were handled by the leadership of the Church, as was demonstrated by the first council found in the book of Acts. Still, never did any of the leaders see any Christian person or group as belonging to a different sect of Christianity. Those that were heretics were dealt with as such; however, all Christians were seen as being from the same Church, the one Church, the one Body of Christ.

Paul's response to this lays bare a very important concept. *"Has Christ been divided?"* The importance of that question is that Paul has seen the Church as Jesus in the earth. We, the Church, are the representation of Jesus in the earth. Indeed! Was not Christ "the Apostle;" was He not "that Prophet;" was He not "Rabboni" or "Master Teacher;" was He not "the Good Shepherd?" When Jesus ascended on high, He took His mantle of authority and divided it into five different callings. Those callings, when in corporate unity with each other and the congregation, make up the image of Christ on earth.

No longer can one person be all things to all people. **We need each other collegially in order to bring Christ corporately to the world.** If we are the Body of Jesus, then it makes perfect sense that we will have His authority, His love, His giftings, His passions, His anointing, and His offices of ministry in order to demonstrate Him to the world!

> *1 Corinthians 3:1-8 And I, brethren, could not speak to you as to spiritual men, but as to men of flesh, as to babes in Christ. I gave you milk to drink, not solid food; for you were not yet able to receive it. Indeed, even now you are not yet able, for you are still fleshly. For since there is jealousy and strife among you, are you not fleshly, and are you not walking like mere men? For when one says, "I am of Paul," and another, "I am of Apollos," are you not mere men? What then is Apollos? And what is Paul? Servants through whom you believed, even as the Lord gave opportunity to each one. I planted, Apollos watered, but God was causing the growth. So then neither the one who plants nor the one who waters is anything, but God who causes the growth. Now he who plants and he who waters are one; but each will receive his own reward according to his own labor.*

Notice that denominational divisions are based in the flesh, which is marked by strife and jealousy. They were not spiritual men. That means that for unity to come to the Body, we need spiritual souls to bring it. We need people who will see the Church as the Lord's Body and not as their own. Paul talked about his desire to present to Christ a bride without spot or wrinkle. He understood that the Church belonged to Christ, and he was only a steward of her. We need leaders again to see the Church as belonging to Jesus, and that they are privileged to be stewards of her to present her in their generation to Christ as a chaste bride.

We have to challenge the mindsets that have been unchallenged for hundreds of years. We have to quit looking at the Church as an organized chain of command. No one organization can make claims that only they are the true believers. Nevertheless, that is what we see among many church organizations. I invite you to look at the Church as a corporate body of believers all over the world of which we are only a part or member. We can no longer define the Church in terms of denominational titles, but as a whole Body with members who have some disagreements.

The true believers make up the Body of Christ and they exist in many different organizations. There is only one division in the Bible; those who believe and those who don't. Every human being fits into one of those two groups.

What's In A Name?

I don't want to bring reproach upon organizational names as long as we are not defining it as the *Church*. In our society, every organization has to legally have a name and it cannot infringe on another organization's name in order to be a legal not-for-profit organization.

So by necessity, we have different names associated with different organizations. It is when these organizations or the members in it begin to define themselves as *the* Body of Christ to the exclusion of other organizations that division has taken place. Are we not all in desperate need of Jesus to guide us in the operation of His Body? Can we do anything without Him? We, the Body (of Christ), need direction and we get this from the Head, Who is Jesus the Christ.

> **John 15:5 ~KJV~** *...for without me ye can do nothing.*

Divine Direction

Let us ponder this for a moment. Can the members of our body (human) do anything without the direction and control of our head? No, they cannot; at least, not anything constructive. We might find, at times, parts of a person's body that are involuntarily moving, but the result is chaotic and not one of order or design. Therefore, if members of the Body of Christ start doing their own thing rather than submitting to the Head, Jesus, then the result will be a chaotic mishmash of movement with no meaning, order, or purpose.

We can say that the head of our human body is authoritative. It is the command center of our body; it has authority in our body and over our body, and it gives our body movement with purpose and direction. If we look at the Body of Christ, we can apply this same principle. Christ is the Head. He is the command center of the whole Body of Christ.

> *Colossians 1:18 **He is also head of the body, the Church;** and He is the beginning, the first-born from the dead; so that He Himself might come to have first place in everything.*

Since Christ is the Head, then it would only make sense that direction for the movement of the Body of Christ would come from Him.

Faith, Grace, and Gifts

> *Romans 12:3-8 For I say, through the grace given to me, to everyone who is among you, not to think of himself more highly than he ought to think, but to think soberly, as God has dealt to each one a measure of faith. For as we have many members in*

*one body, but all the members do not have the same
function, so we, being many, are one body in Christ,
and individually members of one another. Having
then gifts differing according to the grace that is
given to us, let us use them: if prophecy, let us
prophesy in proportion to our faith; or ministry, let
us use it in our ministering; he who teaches, in
teaching; he who exhorts, in exhortation; he who
gives, with liberality; he who leads, with diligence;
he who shows mercy, with cheerfulness.*

Here we see a pattern as to the government of God's
Church. The first thing mentioned is for each of us not to think
more highly of ourselves than we ought to think. This is a very
important statement, especially when there are so many who do
suppose of themselves a higher position than they ought. We must
remember that any talents or gifts that we have are come down
from the Father of lights, Who gives good gifts unto His children.
In spite of this, it is very easy for us to begin to think of these gifts
as something for which we can take credit. We must be on guard
not to take recognition for the gifts we are given, rather let the gifts
work through us so that the glory goes to the Father and not to us.

Next, it says to think with sober judgment, each according
to the measure of faith which God has assigned him. Faith is not
supposed to be a static quality. It is to be dynamic in an increasing
measure in our lives. How many times did Jesus liken faith to a
mustard seed? In that picture of a mustard seed we see growth.
Another important point here is that you cannot manufacture faith.
Faith is first given by God and is measured out by Him. Then, once
we have the seed of faith, it is up to us to grow our faith in order to
produce more seeds of faith. Hence, we are going to have people
that are at different levels of faith.

Also, God allots grace according to what He has called you to do. What I mean by grace is the amalgamation of anointing, gifts, talents, and the immeasurable quality of charisma given by God to an individual to accomplish His purposes in and through their lives. Consequently, someone that is called to have a large ministry will have the amount of grace that it will take to accomplish that call. To a person God has called to write books, He has allotted grace to cover that call.

Accordingly, the picture we get from this is that you are to think of yourself in terms of your calling. You should recognize that what you have is from God and does not germinate from you. In doing this, you realize you cannot judge others based upon what you have, but rather what God has given them. The reason for this is that their callings are different and require different levels of grace to accomplish them.

The next thing the text covers is the concept that we are members of a Body and because of that we are members of one another. Now members serve the Body and the Body serves the members. Members are instruments to be used for God's purpose to accomplish His will for the whole of the Body. Having illustrated this point, Paul goes on to point out our differences when he says, *"Having gifts that differ according to the grace given to us, let us use them..."* We must remember that we all function differently in the Body, and we must remember that we are not to despise any other members for they have their purpose and are hopefully operating according to God's calling, too.

The list that Paul gives is not meant to be all-inclusive. This list includes prophets, ministers or servers, teachers, exhorters, givers, leaders, and those who show mercy. The point behind this is that God has designed each person with certain natural gifts and

He has given certain supernatural gifts for us to fulfill the destiny that He created us to accomplish.

This is an act of His grace and He supplies us a measure of faith to develop in order for us to do His will. With this in mind, we should be sober in our estimation of ourselves, realizing that we are here to bring glory to our Creator and not to ourselves. If we do this, then we will position ourselves to be productive members in the Body.

What About Leaders In The Body?

We also find that there are leaders mentioned in that list. Leaders are called of God to lead and they are endowed with the gifting to do so; therefore, we should submit unto leaders based upon their giftings and level of faith. This is in no way a system of hierarchy. There will be leaders throughout the Body and they are not to be dictators; rather, they are to fulfill the calling of a leader by leading people to their created destiny.

I am taking you through this to show you that we, as a Church, are not structured to have a hierarchical system of government. Many will say that without a chain of command we will have no organizational control; that we will be a mass of confusion and there will be no direction and no accountability. This statement presupposes that Christ is incapable of controlling His Body and bringing His ministers into accountability. We will discuss this in greater detail later, but now I would like to bring clarity to the type of government God has in mind for His people.

What Happened?

What happened? How did the Church go from a collegiate form of government to a hierarchical form of government? I found one piece of evidence that possibly shows that this movement happened very early in church history. In Chapter two of Revelation, we have two mentions of the name "Nicolaitans."

RYRIE STUDY BIBLE COMMENTARY

"The Nicolaitans. Followers of Nicholas (see Acts 6:5), according to the early church fathers. These were apparently a sect which advocated license in matters of Christian conduct, including free love, though some understand from the meaning of the name ('conquering of the people') that they were a group which promoted a clerical hierarchy." [5]

God's Government

Is Jesus so powerless in His own Body that we have to bypass Him as the Head to bring order and direction? Isn't it rather a testament to the power and glory of God that He does not need a single person to accomplish His will; rather, He needs us all at once? Think about that for a moment. What if you have millions of people stationed all around the world, and these people are all part of a corporate body, but there is no human person at the head?

The Corporate Body

In the natural realm, you would have chaos, but if this Body were the Church, then each member would get their orders from God under the oversight of His overseers. No one person knows what the whole is accomplishing; only the Head knows. The Head is orchestrating this great movement of people without

---

[5] *(Ryrie, 1995)*

the need for communication between the different departments. This Head is able to speak to members and arrange for them to accomplish their individual tasks. This is how the Body of Christ was meant to operate. It is the great Providence moving upon a group of people in America to pray for someone in the mission fields of China or a person in Bangladesh being moved upon to pray for the election in the U.S.

> *1 Corinthians 12:12-28 For just as the body is one and has many members, and all the members of the body, though many, are one body, so it is with Christ. For by one Spirit we were all baptized into one body—Jews or Greeks, slaves or free—and all were made to drink of one Spirit. For the body does not consist of one member but of many. If the foot should say, "Because I am not a hand, I do not belong to the body," that would not make it any less a part of the body. And if the ear should say, "Because I am not an eye, I do not belong to the body," that would not make it any less a part of the body. If the whole body were an eye, where would be the hearing? If the whole body were an ear, where would be the sense of smell?*
>
> *But as it is, God arranged the organs in the body, each one of them, as he chose. If all were a single organ, where would the body be? As it is, there are many parts, yet one body. The eye cannot say to the hand, "I have no need of you," nor again the head to the feet, "I have no need of you." On the contrary, the parts of the body which seem to be weaker are indispensable, and those parts of the body which we think less honorable we invest with the greater honor, and our unpresentable parts are*

*treated with greater modesty, which our more
presentable parts do not require.*

*But God has so composed the body, giving the
greater honor to the inferior part, that there may be
no discord in the body, but that the members may
have the same care for one another. If one member
suffers, all suffer together; if one member is
honored, all rejoice together. Now you are the
Body of Christ and individually members of it. And
God has appointed in the church first apostles,
second prophets, third teachers, then workers of
miracles, then healers, helpers, administrators,
speakers in various kinds of tongues.*

Here is the most graphic picture of the Body of Christ in
the entire Bible. This is, without question, the greatest piece of
Scripture concerning this concept. When we read it and understand
it, we come away with a different depiction of how God designed
His corporate Body to operate than what we see functioning today.
Notice what is missing from that section of Scripture. We do not
see any evidence of a single member in authority over all the other
members. There is no hierarchical authority in the members of our
human body other than the head.

The bottom line is that we are all members of this Body,
and *"God has so composed the body, giving the greater honor to
the inferior part, that there may be no discord in the body, but that
the members may have the same care for one another."* This
statement should put all of us in our proper place. God so designed
the Body that it would be in unity, not fighting one another for
positions of power and influence. When you have organizations
that set levels of power, it entices people to attain these levels to
achieve a certain level of recognition. Then you have an

organization that appeals to the base elemental works of our flesh and becomes a feeding ground for it.

The Five Fold Ministry

Our study of the Body of Christ leads us to the purpose and design of the Five Fold Ministry. I will let the Word of God define it and then attempt to expound on what it means. The Five Fold Ministry is God's gift to the Church. It is to be kept intact as it was delivered to us when Jesus gave it to the Church.

> ***Ephesians 4:1-6*** *I therefore, a prisoner for the Lord, beg you to lead a life **worthy** of the calling to which you have been called, with all lowliness and meekness, with patience, forbearing one another in love, eager to maintain the unity of the Spirit in the bond of peace. There is one body and one Spirit, just as you were called to the one hope that belongs to your call, one Lord, one faith, one baptism, one God and Father of us all, who is above all and through all and in all.*

The pattern that Paul shows when he writes about the Body of Christ is that he either begins or ends with how we should treat one another. Paul understood that if people began to look at those with the most gifts, they would bring attention to those people. So Paul's warning is to bear with one another in love, not thinking of ourselves more highly then we ought to.

One thing that stands out to me as I read this scripture is Paul's statement that *"you were called to the one hope that belongs to your call."* Biblical hope is defined as the vision that God has placed on the inside of you that is your call, purpose, and destiny. Everyone in the Body of Christ has a call! If you are in a relationship with God, then I know that God has given you pictures of what He wants you to do. That is hope! Dr. Michael Lake states, *"hope is the blueprint for faith."* This means that God deposited in you hope that becomes a picture that engages your faith to cause the building of your destiny and drive you to the outcome God has planned for you.

> ***Ephesians 4:7-10*** *But grace was given to each of us according to the measure of Christ's gift. Therefore it is said, "When he ascended on high he led a host of captives, and he gave gifts to men." (In saying, "He ascended," what does it mean but that he had also descended into the lower parts of the earth? He who descended is he who also ascended far above all the heavens, that he might fill all things.)*

Each of us has a measure of Christ's gifts in us. These gifts are distributed by the Holy Spirit as He wills. These gifts are all acts of grace in which we have done nothing to deserve them, nor is there anything in us that would cause us to be worthy of them. It is solely on the grace of God that He bestows His gifts on His children and we must always keep this fact in remembrance.

Remember that we discussed grace earlier and revealed that it is the enablement to accomplish God's call. Grace is the conglomeration of anointing, gifts, talents, and charisma given for the effectual working of your call.

> ***Ephesians 4:11-16*** *And his gifts were that some should be apostles, some prophets, some evangelists, some pastors and teachers, to equip the saints for the work of ministry, for building up the Body of Christ, until we all attain to the unity of the faith and of the knowledge of the Son of God, to mature manhood, to the measure of the stature of the fullness of Christ; so that we may no longer be*

*children, tossed to and fro and carried about with
every wind of doctrine, by the cunning of men, by
their craftiness in deceitful wiles. Rather, speaking
the truth in love, we are to grow up in every way
into him who is the head, into Christ, from whom
the whole body, joined and knit together by every
joint with which it is supplied, when each part is
working properly, makes bodily growth and
upbuilds itself in love.*

There are five gifts of ministry mentioned here; they are apostles, prophets, evangelists, pastors, and teachers. This is where we get the term *Five Fold Ministries.* The purpose of these five gifts of ministry is something that needs to be understood so that ministries would begin to model their government structure to follow what the Word says about it.

The text says that these five gifts of ministry were given to equip the saints. What are the saints equipped to do? The work of ministry! This is a far cry from main-stream Christianity today; is it not? What do we see in place today as a rule? We see organizations that are not actively equipping those whom God has given them for the work of ministry. Remember, everyone has a call. The primary function that I see missing in churches today is a systematic training of the saints to do that work of ministry; in other words, discipleship.

We have instead, a congregation that thinks their only duty is to pay tithes and come to church. This is quite a distance from the design of God for His Body. What do you think has brought those in the congregation to the point of thinking these things? Could it be the teaching they have received along with hundreds of years of Church tradition?

What we have in place as a rule are churches that teach their people to bring others into their building on one of the nights they are open in order that they might get saved. This is only one aspect of equipping. It would be better if we were training saints in how to make disciples of Christ in their everyday life. This is the purpose of the ministry; to equip the saints to do the work of ministry. The saints should be equipped to lead people to faith in Christ outside the Church.

The five gifts of ministry are also given for building up the Body of Christ, *"until we all attain to the unity of the faith and of the knowledge of the Son of God, to mature manhood, to the measure of the stature of the fullness of Christ."* Now think again about a human body. How does a human body get built up? It takes proper nourishment, exercise or resistance training, and rest.

Every member of the body has a part in this. Moreover, in accomplishing this we find that there is unity in the body. So it is with the Body of Christ; there must be nourishment upon the Word of God. There must be training that produces action upon that Word which completes faith; this is the exercise. The result is that you will enter into the rest of God in an increasing measure.

If you are someone that has a picture on the inside of what God has called you to do, and you are in a place where you are not getting the nourishment, exercise, and rest that you should, then it is time for you to take a good hard look as to why. Have you talked to your leaders about it? Afterward, do what you can to correct the parts that are wrong. We must all scrutinize our own lives to see if they are positioned under the rule of God. This does not bypass the leadership ministries, but focuses us toward them for that direction. For if they are placed by God in the Body as a leader then we need to access them for the purpose they were ordained to fulfill.

The purpose of all of this is so that the Body of Christ will not be deceived by false teachers. It is imperative that we follow this model given to us by God. If we do not, the result will be the loss of God's presence and the deception of our hearts and minds.

God Our King

Look at the historical accounts of how God has dealt with man and how Satan has interfered. Whose rule was Adam under? Wasn't God the One Who Adam was in submission to? Yes, God was the King and who was it that tempted Adam to subvert this arrangement? That's right; Satan came to Eve and deceived her into subverting the rule of God in their lives. Then Adam willfully betrayed his God. Together, they took from God their will to serve Him and started serving themselves, thinking that they could do a better job and gain more power, which in reality caused them to serve Satan.

> **Genesis 3:5** *For God knows that when you eat of it your eyes will be opened, and you will be like God, knowing good and evil.*

Rebellion

You can see how Satan appealed to the flesh and to self-rule. In short, Adam and Eve rebelled against the government of God over their lives. God wanted to be their King. Why? Is God some kind of egotist that needs to have someone subservient to Him so that He feels good about Himself? Never! It is because He knows that under His rule man will receive the very best leading, safety, and care. God is loving, merciful, just, truthful, and protecting.

It is not any different than how you feel about your relationship with your children. Would you want them to rebel and decide to run their own lives as children or worse yet, chose the neighborhood alcoholic to be their father? Would you want them to come under the rule of another person? Don't you feel that you are best qualified to direct, heal, and protect your children, as well as give them good gifts and a future? Isn't that feeling or belief based in the truth that no one else will love them like you do? This is God's motive to be our Head! Even so, Adam and Eve plunged all of their offspring into an environment where humanity felt a need to run their own lives and consequently separated us all from God.

Adam was in the presence of God before his fall. God would walk with him in the cool of the evening. What a picture of God's love! God was fellowshipping with His creation and undoubtedly giving Adam instruction and wisdom in the things He desired to teach him. However, when Adam fell, he was separated from God. He was not allowed to ever again enter the Garden to be with God.

The next rebellion came after God separated a nation of people for Him to rule over. He called out a people to be the people of God. God wanted a people that would represent Him to the rest of the world and that would allow Him to rule their lives. They did well for a long time, but eventually they too rebelled. I am speaking, of course, about Israel. Again, God had provided His presence to this people. He dwelt with them; only this time it was in the mountain where He would call for them to gather and hear from Him. Observe how God continually wants to be in our lives.

God had instructed Moses to bring all the people near the mountain where, rather than using Moses to speak to them, God would speak to them Himself. When this was done and God spoke from the mountain, the people were afraid and they told Moses that they did not want this relationship with God. God was too awesome for them. They asked for Moses to be the mediator between themselves and God. God was again rejected and separated from His people.

God instructed Moses to build the Ark of Covenant and to put it inside a tabernacle that was designed to house it. Here God would come and dwell in the tabernacle and speak to a priest who would convey the messages of God to the people. This worked for a while, but the people would reject this, too.

When we look at God's dealing with the nation of Israel, we find a pattern that was to be repeated in the Church as well. Before the kings of Israel, there were the judges of Israel. What is the difference? God did not ordain that Israel should be ruled by a human king. He wanted to be their King. When Israel complained to Samuel the prophet and demanded a human king, God revealed that He was being rejected as their King.

> *1 Samuel 8:6-7 But the thing was displeasing in the sight of Samuel when they said, "Give us a king to judge us." And Samuel prayed to the Lord. The Lord said to Samuel, "Listen to the voice of the people in regard to all that they say to you, for they have not rejected you, but they have rejected Me from being king over them."*

The system of government in place just before this rejection consisted of judges who were collegiate leaders among the people of Israel. Samuel had appointed his sons as judges, but they did not walk in the way of Samuel. They perverted justice, took bribes, and turned aside after dishonest gain. The people of Israel were angry with this and demanded a king. Thus, Samuel was distraught because he was blaming himself for Israel's demand for a king. At any rate, God knew the people's hearts and told Samuel that they were rejecting Him, not Samuel.

This is also a good example of assigning bad leadership. I am sure that Samuel loved his sons and wanted them to walk in the ways of God. All too often we find that parents compromise their scruples when it comes to dealing with their children. Perhaps he thought that if they were appointed as judges they would turn from their wicked ways. It may be that Samuel possibly put his own family above the good of the people and even God. We do not have enough evidence to conclude what it was that caused Samuel to place his sons in that oversight position. Nevertheless, we need to understand what a judge is and see if that will give us insight into the government of the Church.

THE JEWISH ENCYCLOPEDIA

Moreover, the designation "Judges," as well as the account given of their activity in the book in its present form, is inadequate, as the term "judge" was subsequently applied to certain persons who, without being kings, ruled over the whole of Israel like the Kings. This happened, however, only when the people were collected together on extraordinary occasions, as, for instance, in making war upon a common enemy, when the members of several or of a majority of the tribes would place themselves under the leadership of the strong warriors among them; and when the object in view had been accomplished, such leaders returned to the respective spheres of their personal influence. This influence did not extend beyond the bounds of their own tribe or of a few other tribes, though they retained the preeminence they had achieved by their leadership in Yhwh's war. In times of peace, moreover, their activities were chiefly

confined to the judicial functions whence they
derived their title. [6]

God was rejected from being King over His creation. God wanted them to be a picture to the rest of the world what it was like to be under His rule. Samuel told them that a human king would draft their sons and daughters into the King's service. He would also confiscate the peoples' fields and vineyards, and he would tax them of their servants, their animals, and their produce.

Contrast that with God's rule. When God called them to war, it was a victory before they even began. God required no service other than the temple service already established. There would not be excessive taxes to fill the King's coffers. The other nations would have learned how to let God rule them as well and thereby help to usher in peace to the whole world. Nevertheless, the people of Israel rejected God's rule for mere human rule.

We see then that God's form of government was to split authority between the judges. God at all times retained the title of King over Israel. The judges were to be a group who investigated problems and ruled according to God's counsel. No single judge had authority over the other judges. This is also a model for the New Testament Church. God has now set five callings over the Church where He Himself fulfilled those five callings in one Person.

Jesus is King over His Church and He rules through His five callings who supply oversight for the Church. The position of oversight is not the office of apostle, prophet, teacher, pastor, or evangelist; it is the office of bishop. Although, all twelve apostles were also bishops. Bishops are overseers in the Church and

---

[6] *(Jewish Encyclopedia, 1901-1906)*

administer that oversight which brings order to the Church; they are drawn from the offices of the Five Fold ministry.

In the Church we have seen the same rebellion that occurred in the nation of Israel when they cried out for a king. Many in church leadership have set themselves up as kings who are accountable to no one. So, like the nation of Israel, some churches have rejected their King Jesus. As a result, the presence of God has or will leave just as He did with Adam and with Israel. Self-promotion to headship will always lead to the same place; a downward spiral of morality to a place of desperation.

What is it about man that he cannot stand to be ruled by anyone? I think that Israel wanted a human king because they thought they would be in greater control of their lives. Isn't that what it is always about with us? A human king they can collectively overthrow, but who can overthrow God?

We are all selfish individuals who are interested in looking out for ourselves. That is the whole point behind the religion of humanism. Self is the all-important part of happiness and existence to the humanist. Psychologists now tell us that we need to get in touch with self if we are to be happy. Everything is designed toward fulfilling self-desires. Look at any advertisement; what do they appeal to? Is it not to satisfy yourself? This is the root of most, if not all, sin.

Rebellion's Summary

✓ God was rejected by a man and woman who plunged the entire human race under the dominion of the prince and power of the air, and God's presence departed.

✓ Then God chose the nation of Israel and again He was rejected. As that nation became more corrupt, God's presence again departed from the nation as we are told in the tenth chapter of Ezra.

✓ Next, He sent His Son Jesus in the likeness of sinful flesh. Jesus was to be the King. You see God sent Himself as a man. He did this as a testimony against us because if man really wanted a man like themselves to rule, then surely they would accept Him because He was also God. Even so, He knew that He would be rejected, but He was rejected as God, not just as a man. This was so the truth of the matter would be known that man was in rebellion and did not want to be ruled by God or by man. It really had nothing to do with having a man rule over them in the first place and by coming to them in the form of a man, He proved that point once and for all. Yet again, the rulers of that nation rejected and even killed the God/man Jesus, Who was come to be their King. Again, God departed from Israel when Jesus ascended into heaven.

✓ In killing Jesus, they ushered in the plan of God to become the Ruler of all humanity again. This time God was to be King over His Church, a collective body of people who believed on Jesus and accepted Him as their King to rule and save them, and they were scattered around the world and in every nation, tribe, and kindred. This time God would send His Holy Spirit to dwell inside each one of them to give them direction; this is where we are today. The presence of God is in each of us who have given control of our lives up to Him. No longer is it a nation of people with a geographical location, rather it is individuals in many different nations who would surrender themselves to the direction of Jesus, Who is the King of this group. At any rate, some still rebel against this in the Church.

Why, then, do we see an active movement within churches to dethrone our King? It is because man wants to have control. Hear this: we have seen a pattern with history that states God will not resist man's attempt to gain control of his own life, but He will depart from that life with His presence. This means that if you or your church seek to control that which God wants to control, you will lose God's manifest presence in your life and/or your church! If we want the manifest presence of God, then we must be willing, as workers in His kingdom, to let God rule our lives and our ministries.

I am not saying that if you rebel against God's authority the indwelling Holy Spirit will leave you. What I am saying is that the glory or manifest presence of God, the tangible presence of God, will leave. It will not only leave us individually if we rebel, but it will leave us corporately if we rebel corporately.

Arguments Used For Hierarchy

We must look at the arguments that have been used to promote a system of hierarchy in the Church. I will not list every argument, but I will list the most viable. First among these arguments is the following Scripture:

> *1 Corinthians 12:28 And God has appointed in the church, first apostles, second prophets, third teachers, then miracles, then gifts of healings, helps, administrations, various kinds of tongues.*

It is argued that this list of three of the five gift ministries enumerated by Paul is given in succession of rank or ranking authority. This means that the list is hierarchical with the apostle as the highest ranking member, the prophet is next in rank, and the teacher is last.

On the surface this may look solid. The Greek really doesn't answer anything because the word "first" can mean both first in rank and first in time. I believe it is first in time, or importance, from the stand point of necessity for the following reason. If it were a chain of command, why is there the absence of the pastor and the evangelist? Have they no rank at all? Also, why is there the inclusion of gifts of healing, helps, administrations, and tongues? Do these gifts have rank above the pastor or evangelist? Why would Paul give us a chain of command and include those spiritual gifts in the list? Can a gift be a leader in the Church?

It would appear to me that because this is the same Paul who wrote Ephesians 4:11, where he revealed the five gift ministries given to the Church, that he would not have left them absent in this list if it were his intention for a chain of command. This list appears to be a list of importance and necessity from an aspect of time.

✓ Apostles build churches; therefore, one cannot have a church unless an apostle has been sent to build it. As Paul said to the Corinthians, *"you are my seal of apostleship."* He meant that because the Corinthian church existed and Paul started it, that was the seal or proof that verified Paul's apostleship.

✓ The Church also needs the prophet to give the Church direction. Without this gift people lack corporate vision and individual vision. Without vision the Church becomes static and in some cases even collusive.

✓ Third in importance are teachers, who are to bring depth of understanding in the Church. If there were no apostles, there would be no one to teach. If there were no prophets, there would be no vision, and even though a teacher could teach, it would be to what end? When a person has a vision, that vision gives them the hunger to pursue it, thus teaching is purposeful.

✓ Then there are the gifts of miracles, healings, helps, administrations, and notice the gift that is listed last. It is the gift of tongues. Why? This focuses back to the Corinthian church which was putting the greater import on tongues. Paul was bringing them back into order concerning what was important.

Let us move on to the next Scripture.

Ephesians 2:19-20 So then you are no longer strangers and aliens, but you are fellow citizens with the saints, and are of God's household, having been built on the foundation of the apostles and prophets, Christ Jesus Himself being the corner stone...

This particular Scripture, when read in context, actually supports my point of collegiate authority. If you read this whole chapter, you will find that Paul is lamenting the fact that the Church is beginning to divide along the teachings of Paul, Apollos, Cephas, and Christ. What Paul is trying to say is that there is no difference in the teachings of these saints and Christ; rather Christ is the Chief Cornerstone.

He laid down the doctrines of the Church for His apostles. His apostles took Christ's teachings and continued to build the foundation level of the Church. Paul was talking about building God's Church, not a government.

> *1 Corinthians 3:6-8* *I planted, Apollos watered, but God was causing the growth. So then neither the one who plants nor the one who waters is anything, but God who causes the growth. Now he who plants and he who waters are one; but each will receive his own reward according to his own labor.*

Paul said that he had planted and Apollos watered. Paul then states that the one who plants and the one who waters is nothing, but Christ Who gives the increase is everything. He also states that the one who plants and the one who waters are one. That was the statement which shows that there is no difference in the teachings of these men; they were in fact the same teachings. Now look at verse nine:

> *1 Corinthians 3:9* *For we are God's fellow workers; you are God's field, God's building.*

Notice that Paul states they were God's *fellow* workers. This looks very much like collegiate oversight rather than hierarchal rule. Also, notice the reference to God's building. It is the Church. So the Church (people) are the building and the five fold are the builders, or fellow builders.

> *1 Corinthians 3:10* *According to the grace of God which was given to me, like a wise master builder I laid a foundation, and another is building on it. But each man must be careful how he builds on it.*

This does not look like Paul is saying anything about hierarchy, but rather the importance of each calling offering their gifting to the same purpose. Just like a real building needs a mason, a carpenter, an electrician, a plumber, and a roofer; the Church needs the giftings of the five callings.

The Church was started by Christ, Who is a single person and to Whom is given the status of a single stone. Then the apostles and prophets are a complete layer of stones. They laid the first foundational layer of the Church which is still being built today.

The Cornerstone

There is some confusion over the use of the word *foundation* as it is used here. Certainly, Jesus is the foundation of the Church. Although in the context used here, Jesus is the *cornerstone*, making more sense of the previous statement. In our modern building technology there is little significance to the cornerstone of a building. If a building has one, it is usually some sign that indicates the date the building was built, or some other item of information. Consider the following:

> *"QUOTE"*
>
> *Many buildings in the ancient Middle East were made of cut stone, and lacking the leveling and squaring technologies we currently have, the cornerstone was of utmost importance. The artisans spent a good deal of time preparing the cornerstone that was trimmed square on the two sides that would align its adjoining walls. It would be set with a pan of water on top of it to assure that it was level in all directions as it was set. The walls would then depend entirely for direction and level upon the placement of the cornerstone.*

When considered this way, we see the apostles
and the prophets, not as the foundation of the
Church, but as the beginning of the Church.
Furthermore, that beginning was entirely
dependent upon Jesus. Consequently, every stone
laid upon that foundation (representing Church
growth) becomes dependent upon Jesus Christ,
and its health is predicated by God's Word, also
laid down by the prophets and apostles. [7]

More Evidence

There is still more evidence of collegiate leadership that we have yet to mine. This area of study is the priesthood. During the rule of Greece and Rome over the nation of Israel, the scribes of Israel translated the Hebrew Scriptures into Greek. This work is called the Septuagint and was available when Jesus walked this earth. The importance of this work is tremendous. The reason for this is that we can look up a Greek word in the Septuagint and reverse translate it into Hebrew. To expose the import of this work consider the following:

> *Numbers 4:16 ~KJV~ And to the **office** of Eleazar*
> *the son of Aaron the priest pertaineth the oil for the*
> *light, and the sweet incense, and the daily meat*
> *offering, and the anointing oil, and the oversight of*
> *all the tabernacle, and of all that therein is, in the*
> *sanctuary, and in the vessels thereof.*
>
> *Nehemiah 11:22 ~KJV~ The **overseer** also of the*
> *Levites at Jerusalem was Uzzi the son of Bani, the*
> *son of Hashabiah, the son of Mattaniah, the son of*

---

[7] *–American Journal of Biblical Theology*

Micha. Of the sons of Asaph, the singers were over the business of the house of God.

The two words that are highlighted in bold were translated from Hebrew to Greek as *episkopos,* which is translated in the New Testament as "bishop" or "overseer." In the first account, Eleazar is ranked under Aaron the high priest and is called a bishop or overseer. In the second account, we have Uzzi, who is called a bishop. Uzzi was the son of the high priest Bani. What is the significance of this?

It points again to what God designed as His preferred form of government. Presently, Jesus is our High Priest and the Church has only one High Priest forever; under Him is collegiate leadership known as bishops.

We also have evidence that Gideon understood God's desired government for Israel. After Gideon won a tremendous battle against the enemies of Israel, the people began to give the glory of the victory to Gideon. They called for him to become their leader. Let's take a look at Gideon's response.

> *Judges 8:22-23 Then the men of Israel said to Gideon, "Rule over us, both you and your son, also your son's son, for you have delivered us from the hand of Midian." But Gideon said to them, "I will not rule over you, nor shall my son rule over you; the Lord shall rule over you."*

"The Lord shall rule over you!" That was Gideon's response. He understood the rule of God over His people. Now let us go into the Book of Acts and see if there is evidence of collegiate rule in the first New Testament Church.

> *Acts 6:1-2 Now at this time while the disciples were increasing in number, a complaint arose on the part*

of the Hellenistic Jews against the native Hebrews, because their widows were being overlooked in the daily serving of food. So the twelve summoned the congregation of the disciples and said, "It is not desirable for us to neglect the word of God in order to serve tables."

Who was the set leader in this church? The twelve were all in positions of leadership and they with one voice summoned the congregation of disciples. If Jesus intended a hierarchical rule, could we not assume that the apostles would have established that system of government in the first church? We find this more than once in the book of Acts.

Acts 15:2 And when Paul and Barnabas had great dissension and debate with them, the brethren determined that Paul and Barnabas and some others of them should go up to Jerusalem to the apostles and elders concerning this issue.

Note the use of the term "apostles and elders." All of the apostles were also elders. This is revealed in the failure of Judas Iscariot. It is said in the book of Acts, *"Let another take his office"* or as the King James puts it, *"His bishoprick let another take."* This word "bishoprick" is that Greek word *episcope* which means "elder." From this we can deduce that the twelve were all elders or overseers of the church at Jerusalem.

It could not be any clearer that God desires to be the Head of His Church and that the apostles understood this, shepherding the flock with oversight not lording over them. If we adopt this type of rule again, we can become the Church that Jesus announced would advance His kingdom!

Accountability

All of this raises the question: *"If the Church government is collegiate, rather than hierarchical, what about accountability?"* Let me say this; we do have accountability. In fact it is greater accountability then the hierarchal model can offer. It is sideways accountability in the physical realm and upward accountability in the spiritual realm. (Christ is the Head.) God's ministers were to be rulers, but they were not to lord over the flock (Body) of Christ.

> ***Mark 10:42-45*** *And calling them to Himself, Jesus said to them, "You know that those who are recognized as rulers of the Gentiles lord it over them; and their great men exercise authority over them. But it is not so among you, but whoever wishes to become great among you shall be your servant; and whoever wishes to be first among you shall be slave of all. For even the Son of Man did not come to be served, but to serve, and to give His life a ransom for many."*

We get the idea from this section of Scripture that those who want to be great must become a servant in God's government. Even though this is a position of authority, it is marked by servitude. Still, there will be times that we will have to deal with a bad leader. This next section provides a biblical framework for dealing with bad leadership.

Dealing With Bad Leadership

What is a church to do when there is a bad leader? First, if there is collegiate leadership, the other leaders are in a position to deal with the bad leader. We also have an example in the Bible of a corrupt and unruly leader.

*3 **John 9-10** I wrote something to the church; but Diotrephes, who loves to be first among them, does not accept what we say. For this reason, if I come, I will call attention to his deeds which he does, unjustly accusing us with wicked words; and not satisfied with this, neither does he himself receive the brethren, and he forbids those who desire to do so, and puts them out of the church.*

At this point in history, John is the last living of the twelve apostles. If there were a special authority from a hierarchical sense, he would have dismissed Diotrephes from his duties as a leader. However, we see that the apostle John does not seek to unseat this person; instead, he says that he will bring attention to his works. This shows collegiate authority. To whom will he bring attention of this man's deeds? The Body of Christ! He will take this to the Body of Christ, who then, as a collective body of whom Christ is the Head, will be able to submit themselves to the other leaders, thus isolating the bad one.

Imagine having a college of doctors to whom you submit your physical health. If one doctor goes bad, you just continue to submit to the other doctors while the bad doctor is isolated and replaced. John demonstrated his respect for positional authority, yet he was able to isolate this bad leader by appealing to one of the other leaders.

It must be noted that this is not the system of government known as *congregational rule*. Under this system of government the people unseat and remove the leaders that they consider as going astray. This presents a huge problem. The very people who are least able to make mature godly decisions concerning God's Church are placed in the position of doing so. It results in immature believers changing leaders based upon reasons not considered viable. Look what the apostle John does as we continue in this text.

> *3 John 11-12 Beloved, do not imitate what is evil, but what is good. The one who does good is of God; the one who does evil has not seen God. Demetrius has received a good testimony from everyone, and from the truth itself; and we add our testimony, and you know that our testimony is true.*

Notice that John points the local church toward another leader. This is how John handled bad leadership; he basically told the local church to quit following the bad leader and pointed them toward a better one. In handling this problem the way he did, John did not violate positional authority. We are not to govern the Church by a system which has a chain of command. Just as Israel was not to have a king neither is the Church! God wants to be our King!

Lord or Leader

What is the difference between a lord and a leader? In the Greek the word lord is *kurios* (from which we get the word "church"), and it means *he to whom a person or thing belongs, about which he has power of deciding; master, lord; the possessor and disposer of a thing; the owner; one who has control of the person, the master.* So the indication is that of a person who has authority over a person or thing to the extent that they have control over them. This is what we as ministers are ***not*** to be like.

The word "leader" in the Greek is *hegeomai* {hayg-eh'-om-ahee}, and its meaning is *to lead; to go before; to be a leader; overseers or leaders of the churches; to consider, deem, account, think.* "To go before" means that I have done something and learned how and now I am able to teach others how to do it. I have authority, but my authority is not as much over people as it is over the area of my expertise. We see this model at work when Christ was on this earth. What did He do? He made disciples of men. In short, a disciple is a pupil. If they are pupils, then they must have a teacher. Jesus was that Teacher. Jesus told us to make disciples. The pattern is supposed to be repeated so that there would always be a generation of leaders able to lead when they are gone.

Making Disciples

> **Hebrews 13:17** *Obey your leaders and submit to them; for they are keeping watch over your souls, as men who will have to give account. Let them do this joyfully, and not sadly, for that would be of no advantage to you.*

If we look at the word "obey" in the Greek, it is the same word used for "persuade." So its meaning is "to be persuaded of a thing." In other words, you just do not blindly follow someone, but you must be persuaded in your own mind and heart that this is a true man of God and that God has sent you there to learn from them. If you are not persuaded of this person, then you should not submit to him and find someone who is able to persuade you concerning the truth.

First, God must have sent you, and the person must have credibility in your eyes. Then, they must be willing to mentor you. It is not a one-way relationship. The mentor has just as much a right to deny mentoring you as you have to be mentored by another. Next, you submit to him and become his disciple. Once this is done you are not to enter into mentorship with any other. Can you imagine the disciples getting mentored by someone else at the same time as Jesus was their Mentor?

This is what it is all about; Jesus said, *"Go into all the world and make disciples of every nation"* (Matthew 28:19). Therefore, those of us who are called by God into a ministerial office should be making students. Then, some of these students, when matured, will make other students.

I realize that not every student is called to a ministerial office, but every student is called to something, and that something requires training from the five fold ministry to help him in accomplishing God's will for his life. This also speaks to the accountability of the person who is a leader. If a leader is not leading as God has called him to, and if there is collegiate leadership, then your responsibility is to submit to those leaders who have a good testimony and let them deal with the one who is not a good leader.

If you are listening to the Head (Christ), and if everyone else under that leader is listening to the Head, then you will find that the Head will call you away from false teachers. If everyone is listening to Jesus, then they will be drawn toward those who God has established as good leaders and away from the bad ones. When this happens, the bad leaders will be left with no one to lead and accountability has been accomplished.

> *1 **Peter** 5:5 Likewise you younger people, submit yourselves to your elders. Yes, all of you be submissive to one another, and be clothed with humility, for "God resists the proud, But gives grace to the humble."*

We are all to submit ourselves to one another for accountability. Those of us who are ministers are especially to submit to other ministers so that there may be accountability in the Body. It is also important not to undermine nor come against a leader. We must adhere to the example of David, who refused to take the throne by force even after God had anointed him king. Instead, he prayed, and he waited for God to take King Saul out of power. If God is the One Who put King Saul in a place of leadership, then it must be God who takes him out of leadership. This is also true of replacing leaders today; God will do this work.

Your responsibility to your leader when he has gone astray is to pray for him and let God deal with him. God will send him people who are called to restore him. Take your leave of him, if you must, pray for him, but do not come against him. If God has put him in that position, then God will deal with him. If you are found fighting against God's delegated leader, then God will come against you. This is why David waited for God to take King Saul out of power.

Whatever God calls a person to do, He empowers him with the divine authority and grace to get it done. Even if that person has gone into error, there is still a divine authority that rests in the calling of that person. The Bible tells us that God does not take back callings or gifts. This means that you can backslide and still retain your calling and your giftings. The holder of the calling and the giftings is responsible for how he or she carries them out. Be careful, therefore, not to come against someone who God has positioned.

God wants us to govern His Church with a system whereby He retains headship. Yes, God will call people to be in positions of leadership, but not lordship. God will call people to be in positions of authority, but as a servant. Look at Moses; he was called of God to LEAD the people of Israel out of the land of Egypt.

What was Moses supposed to tell the leaders of the tribes of Israel after God had sent him to them? God told Moses to tell the leaders of Israel that He was going to set them free and lead them to a land which flows with milk and honey. God said that the leaders would listen to and accept Moses. Who was in charge here? Who was giving direction? Was it not God Who was leading and directing? Was it not God Who had the ultimate authority? Moses did not lord over the people; he led them. He had authority, but he used it to lead and protect, not manipulate and control.

A Bigger Plan

If we all follow our callings we will be part of a bigger plan that we cannot even see. You are a small part of the Body and just doing what you are called to do creates a living organism of people doing the will of God at once. No single person knows the big picture; each person just knows what he or she is called to do or at most the church organization they are a part of. The hand does not know what the plan is; it only knows the command given to it to operate according to the head. The foot does not know the destination of the whole body; it knows only the direction according to the head. So it is the same with us, and when we act according to our callings, others should recognize and submit to our part and position in the body as we submit to theirs.

What do we observe today? Instead of unity and humility, we have strife and jealousy which creates competition and division in the Body of Christ. One foot is trying to beat the other foot; one hand is trying to beat the other hand. Many in the Body of Christ are measuring success by numbers rather than obedience. It should be our aspiration that our brothers and sisters in Christ should exceed our own ministries. After all, isn't the goal to win souls, feed the poor, visit the fatherless, help the widow, and expand the kingdom of God? If this is the goal, why are we trying to beat others rather than support them?

The ultimate authority over the Church belongs to the Head alone. The followers, as a collective Body (the Church), should submit to the Head's leadership team. They would also reject those that are false leaders.

> **Luke 22:27** *"For who is greater, the one who reclines at the table, or the one who serves? Is it not the one who reclines at the table? But I am among you as the one who serves."*

I ask you, *"Who is serving and who is eating?"* Is it not the minister who is serving the Word of God and the others are being served? So, who is greater? It is those who are hearing and receiving the Word!

I don't think our system of church government is as effective as it could be. The Bible tells us that we have pastors, evangelists, prophets, apostles, and teachers given for equipping the saints to do the work of God. Presently, however, most churches today have a top down rule.

What would excite me is to see each minister being subject to the gifts of other ministers. I would like to see the assembly taught and admonished to do the work they are called to do with in-house training and support. There is a wealth of talent and calling going to waste in the pews because the leaders do not trust the work of the Holy Spirit in the lives of those in their care. It is kind of like the I-always-want-to-drive-because-I-feel-safer syndrome. Are they going to make mistakes? Yes. Who of us in our ministries has not made a mistake?

I would admonish us all to submit to others' gifts and callings so that the Body would be built up and in need of nothing. My foot submits to the work of my hand and vice versa; they do not try to switch callings, rather they complement each other in the task of completing the job.

They also do not compete with each other; rather, they support each other. It is like when you can't hear well enough with your ears, your hand comes to the rescue and cups itself around the ear to enhance the hearing according to the direction of the head. Shouldn't it be this way with us as well? Each of us goes about the business of the head's instructions. The foot does not say to the hand, *"Hey, get out of here; I can do your job!"* My whole body works together for good. We should see ourselves as enhancing others in their ministries.

God did not leave us without direction; He sent us His Holy Spirit. Nevertheless, the Church today seems somewhat afraid to rely on this precious gift. It is essential, however, that we learn to rely on Him for He will lead us and guide us into all truth. In this, we will know those among us who are false. Our spirits will not bear witness with them. We must be careful here. We cannot bring accusations against an elder without the witness of two or three people. I want you to understand what a high standard this is. Unless there are at least two eye witnesses to an infraction by a leader, there is to be no accusation.

Thus, we observe that the collective fellowship in the Spirit (the Body of Christ) will collectively excommunicate those who are not sent of God because our spirits will not bear witness with those who are false. By the way, this witness can only take place in the atmosphere of submission, else we will be deceived. The government of God's kingdom is not upheld by any one human being, but by the fellowship of the saints in the Holy Spirit. *"Not by power or might, but by my Spirit says the Lord"* (Zechariah 4:6).

We will also see that we can tell false leaders by their fruits. That means we can tell their purpose by what people do in consistent action. Why is it when we actually do this we are told that we are judging, implying we should not? To judge means simply to form an opinion or estimation of after careful consideration. That is, you determine right from wrong and react accordingly. We all do this every day, and we must.

> *Matthew 7:15-20* *"Beware of the false prophets, who come to you in sheep's clothing, but inwardly are ravenous wolves. You will know them by their fruits. Grapes are not gathered from thorn bushes, nor figs from thistles, are they? Even so, every good tree bears good fruit; but the bad tree bears bad fruit. A good tree cannot produce bad fruit, nor can a bad tree produce good fruit. Every tree that does not bear good fruit is cut down and thrown into the fire. So then, you will know them by their fruits."*

From this we can see that we are to judge the actions of those who call themselves sheep but are not. This is really important. No matter how likable a person is, we have to look carefully at their actions. Doing so can be painful to us, but it is imperative that we do and that we couple this with what the Spirit of God is telling us in our hearts in congruence with the Word of God. Jesus said that we would know them by their actions; we know the Bible tells us that from the abundance of the heart the mouth speaks (Matthew 12:34).

If the action is consistently foul, so is the heart. It is that simple. If the actions are consistently and purposely hurtful, so is the heart. If the reaction is consistently selfish, so is the heart. Whatever the deeds, the heart is made transparent by them; this is not known by a single deed, but of a collection of them.

Praise God for His wonderful instruction! According to Psalm 23, we are the sheep in His care; He will let us rest in the green pastures; He will restore our soul; He will lead us beside the still waters; He will guide us in paths of righteousness; He gives us courage in times of despair; He comforts us; He prepares a meal for us in the presence of our enemies; He anoints our heads with oil; He fills our cups to overflowing and He gives us His love and goodness. How can we fail when we have such a great Lover of our souls leading us into truth?

Summation

In closing this chapter we need to realize the ramifications of false church government and true church government. False church government is marked by the eventual departure of God's manifest presence and power. True church government is marked by the possession of God's manifest presence and power.

It must be concluded that God did not establish a hierarchical form of government over His Body; rather, He has established a college of leaders to oversee the operation of His Body. There will be times that a leader will follow the course of this world and will need to be corrected. How much easier would it be on the Body if they are under the rule of a college of leaders rather than one leader?

Let us close this chapter with a heart-felt prayer for the restoration of true government within churches and the recognition of each ministry according to how the Head has placed them. Let us not be in opposition to leadership, but rather recognize and reward those among us who have proven themselves by their works that they are true leaders.

Let us, who are leaders, return to true leadership as servants, and let us abandon lordship. Let us recognize the value of those God has entrusted to us that we might serve them with the same dedication as Christ Himself would. Let us pray that God's rule, presence, and power return to a triumphant Church to proclaim the good news.

From here, we need to transition from the government of God to the leadership of God. What I mean by that is that we need to seek what kind of leader we are to be in God's kingdom. We also need to be willing to receive God's choice of leaders among us so that we will be found to be in submission to God's rule from heaven. In looking at God's chosen leaders there are two gifts that stand out as having been removed from the consciences of the people of God. We will deal first with reestablishing these two callings to their proper place.

Becoming a Judge

Chapter Three

If we are to understand the ministry under the New Testament Covenant, we are going to have to understand the judge as revealed in the Old Covenant. If God's preferred government in the Old Covenant is the period of the judges and the preferred government of God in the future kingdom is that of the judges, then I think we can safely conclude that there is an element of judge in the understanding of the New Covenant minister.

The word "judge" is a compound word from the Latin *judicare*. The Latin *jus* mean "right" or "law" and *dicere* which means "to decide" or "say." Therefore we could say it means "to speak law," "to speak right," "to decide law," or "to decide right." That is a pretty good picture of what a judge is or does.

There is a level of interpretation that is done at the letter level in the Hebrew language. The reason is that each letter is a picture and when you put pictures together you can tell a story. Having revealed the etymology of the word "judge" let us see if it is a good translation from the Hebrew.

The Hebrew letters for the word "judge" are these three pictures: teeth, mouth, and support or prop up. We see in these pictures the action of saying and supporting. The law is meant to support the righteous and punish the wicked. Thus, the word "judge" is indeed speaking or deciding rightly. To what could we compare this in the New Testament?

The Greek word for "judge" is *krino* and this means first to separate and then to select or decide. Here we see that the judge

Page | 80

has to separate fact from fiction and decide based upon their findings.

episkope.

1. This first came into common use in the LXX. In the only instance in secular Greek it means a. "visit." In the LXX, however, it means b. "look," "glance," c. "care," "protection," d. "inquiry," and e. "muster." f. There is no equivalent for the verb "to miss," passive "to be missing." g. The true theological sense is when the term is used for "visitation." **More weakly it denotes judicial punishment in Lev. 19:20, but mostly it is used for divine visitation in judgment, as in Num. 16:29; Dt. 28:25.** *Disobedient nations will be visited by God (Jer. 6:15). Their idols will be broken on the day of visitation (Is. 10:3). Thunder and earthquake will accompany the final visitation (Is. 29:6). h. But the divine visitation may also be in mercy and grace, as in Gen. 50:24-25; Is. 23:16. i. The meaning "office" also occurs in a transition from more general "oversight" to official responsibility (Num. 4:16; Ps. 109:8, where the Hebrew may mean "goods," but the LXX, followed by Acts 1:20, has episkopḗ in the sense of "office").*[8]

LXX Septuagint

[8]Kittel, G., Friedrich, G., & Bromiley, G. W. (1995, c1985). *Theological dictionary of the New Testament.* Translation

There is no question as to the connection of the bishop to that of judging. This means that we should see more evidence along this line that God has called bishops to be the overseers or judges of the Church.

In John 21:15-17 Jesus admonished Peter three times. Two times He tells Peter to *"Feed my lambs"* and *"Feed my sheep."* Once He tells Peter to *"Shepherd my sheep."* Now note the following:

> **Jeremiah 3:15** *"Then I will give you shepherds after My own heart, who will feed you on knowledge and understanding."*

The next question would be, *"Is there a connection between shepherding and being a bishop?"*

> **Acts 20:28** *"Be on guard for yourselves and for all the flock, among which the Holy Spirit has made you **overseers**, to **shepherd** the Church of God which He purchased with His own blood."*

Who was Paul speaking with? According to verse seventeen he had called the elders of that church. This means that there is not only a connection between being a shepherd and bishop, but an elder as well. With regard to church government that we often see today, the board of elders are not the shepherds but congregants. This would not be a correct form of government. Is there any other connection like this in the Bible?

> *1 **Peter 5:2 shepherd** the flock of God among you, exercising **oversight** not under compulsion, but*

---

of: Theologisches Worterbuch zum Neuen Testament. (245). Grand Rapids, Mich.: W.B. Eerdmans.

voluntarily, according to the will of God; and not for sordid gain, but with eagerness.

Here again we find the same two terms, shepherding and oversight. Only in this section Peter uses the verb form of overseer rather than the noun. The meaning is the same as Acts 20:28. We have to ask the question again though, *"Who was Peter talking to?"* Verse one has the answer.

*1 **Peter** 5:1Therefore, I exhort the **elders** among you, as your fellow elder and witness of the sufferings of Christ, and a partaker also of the glory that is to be revealed...*

Again, shepherding, elder, and bishop are all synonymous. Both Apostles Paul and Peter used the same terminology. What can we take from this? I think we can deduce from this that the elder refers to a level of spiritual maturity. This was always the case in many different communities and it was called elder because of the age that one has in relation to the time it takes to become spiritually mature.

The bishop refers to the judge. This is a seat of authority. Note that eldership or spiritual maturity is assumed if one was to become a judge. Bishop is a position rather than a condition.

Finally, the shepherd refers to the fruit or action of ministry toward the Church. Shepherding is the work or action. So we conclude the following.

- Elder is a condition of spiritual maturity
- Bishop is a position like the judge
- Shepherd is the action it produces upon the Church
- Calling is the passion and special gifting

All four can be the same person. It explains their position and the qualifications to function in it. This is a picture of the kind of leaders that were selected to oversee a church. Of the five callings, one could be selected to be a bishop because they are an elder to oversee and shepherd a local church. It does not matter which calling is selected. I see no evidence to support an elder who is not from the five gift ministries.

The Elder

It is important to note that elder is more of a condition than it is a position. Note the following verse.

> *Luke 22:66 When it was day, the **Council of elders** of the people assembled, both chief priests and scribes, and they led Him away to their council chamber, saying...*

Notice that the council of elders is actually made up of chief priests and scribes. So elder is a term that reflects a place of leadership based upon the acquisition of maturity by age.

> *Acts 14:23 When they had **appointed elders** for them in every church, having prayed with fasting, they commended them to the Lord in whom they had believed.*

Note that elders are appointed, although elder is not a position. This just means that to be appointed one must be an elder, but what they were appointed to was the office of overseer. Compare this with calling. A calling is given by God and is a gift, whereas elder is a spiritual condition attained through maturity. Elders are then able to become bishops who are selected and appointed to oversee the church. This shows us that apostles, prophets, teachers, pastors, and evangelists can operate in their calling without being an elder or bishop. The appointments, however, are not likely to have been novice Christians.

Some have even made the argument that elders are not drawn from the five fold, but this verse is not the proof. Because they do not identify who these elders are, it cannot prove that they were not from the ministry no more than it can prove that they were. Note that Paul states to Timothy that the selection of bishops are not to be novices. Where then could they have drawn elders from? It is more likely that they were taken from the Jewish Synagogue where they were very aware of and schooled in the Scriptures.

There are many times that the term "apostles and elders" are used. This is not a suggestion that elders were not from the ministry. Many times elder is used in this way even though the others were elders as well. The twelve apostles were also elders.

> *1 Timothy 5:17-19 The **elders** who rule well are to be considered worthy of double honor, especially those who work hard at preaching and teaching. For the Scripture says, "YOU SHALL NOT MUZZLE THE OX WHILE HE IS THRESHING," and "The laborer is worthy of his wages." Do not receive an accusation against an elder except on the basis of two or three witnesses.*

From this we see that elders preach and teach. This is an equipping ministry at work. Again, I am not saying that all five fold ministers are elders, but that they are chosen from the body of ministers available. There is also the admonition that elders should not be too easily accused. There must be two or more witnesses before an accusation can take place. Why? It is assumed that if one has become an elder they have already demonstrated by their life, integrity, honesty, and a fear of God, else they would not have that position.

> *James 5:14 Is anyone among you sick? Then he must call for **the elders of the church** and they are to pray over him, anointing him with oil in the name of the Lord.*

Why the elders of the church? If the elders were just congregants and not ministers, why would James point them out to be the ones to pray for the sick in the congregation? Elders are not only elders, they are bishops, they are pastors, they are apostles, they are teachers, they are prophets, and they are evangelists.

> *1 Peter 5:1 Therefore, I exhort the **elders** among you, as your **fellow elder** and witness of the sufferings of Christ, and a partaker also of the glory that is to be revealed...*

First, it must be noted that Peter reveals to his readers that he is an elder. This is an admonition for his fellow elders to do something. First, if they are "fellow" elders than that assumes perhaps a position of ministry as well. Again, every time an elder is identified, it is a person with a ministry gift. What was the admonition?

> *1 Peter 5:2 **shepherd the flock of God among you, exercising oversight** not under compulsion, but voluntarily, according to the will of God; and not for sordid gain, but with eagerness.*

Congregants do not shepherd the flock of God, they are the flock of God. According to the wording of this verse all elders are in a place to exercise oversight. This points back to the bishop again. Shepherding is a ministerial function of the five fold ministry. We could deduce then that elders are also bishops or overseers as the NASB renders it.

> *2 John 1 The elder to the chosen lady and her children, whom I love in truth; and not only I, but also all who know the truth...*

Here the Apostle John reveals himself as an elder. John is also an apostle; John is also a bishop. John is Elder-Bishop-Apostle John. Elder reveals John's maturity. Bishop reveals John's office of oversight as judge. Apostle reveals John's gift and passion for the Body of Christ.

The Bishop or Overseer

The bishop is again much like a judge. They visit, investigate, and judge matters within the local church. This is not a gift in itself. Gifts are employed in the function of this office, but the office itself is not a gift.

> *1 Timothy 3:1 It is a trustworthy statement: if any man aspires to the office of overseer, it is a fine work he desires to do.*

That word "aspire" in the Greek means "to reach for." This reveals that the office of bishop is something that can be attained or reached for. Calling, on the other hand, is not negotiable. Jesus did not negotiate with His disciples, he named them apostles. You cannot choose which calling God calls you to, but you can choose whether to function in the office of bishop. This reveals a clear and distinct difference between the five callings and the office of bishop.

Notice also that there are no qualifications given for being an apostle, prophet, pastor, evangelist, or teacher. These are callings upon a person that begins at conception. Because one cannot aspire to any of these callings, there are no qualifications for them. It is more of who a person is based upon their created purpose. Any office that one can aspire to would also have certain qualifications that must be met. This is the case for the bishop.

> **1 Timothy 3:2** *An overseer, then, must be above reproach, the husband of one wife, temperate, prudent, respectable, hospitable, able to teach,,,*

As we begin looking at the qualifications for a bishop, the first one mentioned is to be "above reproach." This qualification would point to the past in a person's life. It means that they have conducted their life in such a way that there are no accusations against them. They come to the office with no scandals.

Next, the bishop must be the husband of one wife. This has been the subject of much debate for many years. Does the author mean one wife at a time or one in a lifetime? I think we can deduce which one is intended by the author. First, the culture was replete with husbands who had plurality of wives. All this means is that if Paul did intend to address polygamy there is the evidence of such that would warrant this kind of a statement.

This verse has been used many times to disqualify a minister who had gone through a divorce no matter what the circumstances of it were. Here is the problem I have with this verse meaning one wife in a lifetime. If we are to accept this on face value, then not only would a person who went through a divorce automatically be disqualified if they were to remarry, it would also disqualify a widower who remarried later.

We know this could not be true based upon Paul's treatment of it in Romans chapter seven. In this chapter Paul describes how when a spouse dies the surviving spouse is released from the law and is now able to be joined to another. It is because of this that I believe 1 Timothy 3:2 is dealing only with polygamy.

The bishop must be temperate, which means that they are to have a level of sobriety that denotes a life apart from the use of alcohol. If one is to be in the place of judging they must have all of their faculties in the exercise of their office.

Prudence is the quality of being rational. One cannot be a judge of anything without rationality. One must be able to look at all sides and rationalize a just decision. Without this quality, decisions would be rendered in a mish mash of feelings rather than on the facts.

Respectable means that you have proven yourself in the company of others to be trustworthy and honest. You deal fairly with people and this produces a trust that causes them to see you as worthy of it.

Hospitable behavior is the ability to make others feel comfortable in your presence. You are unassuming, unpretentious, and congruent in your dealings with others.

Able to teach means that the person will have the ability to equip others with the knowledge of God. This also points to the fact that they are harvested from the five gift ministries mentioned in Ephesians 4:11-12. This does not suggest that a person not of these five is not able to teach, but if one is to be a bishop they must have that as a quality in their life.

1 Timothy 3:3 3 not addicted to wine or pugnacious, but gentle, peaceable, free from the love of money.

Again, we have mentioned the problem of alcohol. Note that Aaron the high priest had two sons who functioned as priests under him who offered strange fire and were killed by God for their offering. It was after this event that the prohibition of alcohol was instituted in the functioning of priestly duties.

Gentleness is the absence of arrogance and pomp. It is a quality usually displayed by someone that is comfortable in their own skin. They feel no need to impress others or receive accolades from their peers.

To be peaceable means that one is not easily provoked to brawling. I have seen some leaders that were always right on the edge of a fight. It usually did not take much to tip them to lose control.

There should be a lack of the love of money. That simply means that one should not be in the position for the money. That does not mean that they should not be compensated, but that they have a passion for the job that transcends compensation.

> *1 Timothy 3:4-5 He must be one who manages his own household well, keeping his children under control with all dignity (but if a man does not know how to manage his own household, how will he take care of the church of God?)*

The bishop should have displayed management skills since he will be in charge of managing the church or churches under his care. This would also show good judgment which will be necessary to function in this office.

> *1 Timothy 3:6 and not a new convert, so that he will not become conceited and fall into the condemnation incurred by the devil.*

This next qualification is one that causes some to suggest that this office is not associated only to the five callings. However, we must understand that a new convert is not synonymous with youth. You could have an elderly person that has all of these qualities and yet be just saved. I have seen so many good people destroyed simply because they had a name, but were a new convert that was thrust into a leadership role.

> *1 Timothy 3:7 And he must have a good reputation with those outside the church, so that he will not fall into reproach and the snare of the devil.*

Not only is the candidate to be one who has demonstrated good relations with fellow believers, but they must also demonstrate that they are able to function in the company of unbelievers.

This list of qualifications is impressive. It shows that there is a real difference between being a bishop and being a minister. There is a rabbinical term that also points to the bishop. It is "bet din" and it means court house. In England during the twelfth and thirteenth century they had a title called Bishop of the Jews and this position corresponded to the bet din. Next, let's take a closer look at the judge.

The Judge

So far we have laid a case for the preferred government of God being that of the King Himself ruling on earth through judges. We see this in the Old Covenant and the New Kingdom, but what about the New Testament? If God does not change and He plans to rule the way He wants, then we should see some evidence that this is for the Church age as well.

Note that when man rejected God for a human king, God became a human King. By doing this He reinstates Himself as King over His people. That King now rules from heaven over His

Church and will soon come to this earth to rule over all the nations. I am inclined to believe that God wants the government of the Church to look just like the government of the Old Testament and the government of the new kingdom.

> *1 Corinthians 5:1-3 It is actually reported that there is immorality among you, and immorality of such a kind as does not exist even among the Gentiles, that someone has his father's wife. You have become arrogant and have not mourned instead, so that the one who had done this deed would be removed from your midst. For I, on my part, though absent in body but present in spirit, have **already judged him** who has so committed this, as though I were present.*

The Apostle Paul saw it as his duty to judge a member of the Corinthian church. He expected this judgment to have come from within that local church. Note the phrase "as though I were present." Paul saw this as a duty from within the local church.

> *1 Corinthians 5:12 For what have I to do with judging outsiders? Do you not judge those who are within the church?*

Paul does put some restrictions on this concept. Bishops are to judge people inside the church, but are not to judge people outside the church. These matters of judgment are dealing with sin, as in this case, and with doctrine, but not salvation. There are some other restrictions.

> *Colossians 2:16-17 Therefore no one is to act as your judge in regard to food or drink or in respect to a festival or a new moon or a Sabbath day—*

things which are a mere shadow of what is to come;
but the substance belongs to Christ.

Judgment is not meant for food, ceremony, or days. That is, that we are not to judge one group because they choose to have church service on Sunday rather than Saturday. These things are not to be the focus of our judgment. Again, it is restricted to sin and doctrine. I find it disheartening that for the most part many churches no longer judge sin or doctrine, but they do judge procedure.

> *1 Corinthians 6:2-4 Or do you not know that the*
> *saints will judge the world? If the world is judged*
> *by you, are you not competent to constitute the*
> *smallest law courts? Do you not know that we will*
> *judge angels? How much more matters of this life?*
> *So if you have law courts dealing with matters of*
> *this life, do you appoint them as judges who are of*
> *no account in the church?*

Paul actually commends the establishment of small law courts within the church with appointed judges. Who were these judges to be? I argue that they are elder-bishop-called ones. Who are the appointed positions? The only appointed positions are those that have requirements associated with them. They are the bishop and the deacon.

> *Matthew 5:1-2 When Jesus saw the crowds, He*
> *went up on the mountain; and after He sat down,*
> *His disciples came to Him. He opened His mouth*
> *and began to teach them, saying...*

I include these verses to set up the audience Jesus is speaking to. This will bring clarity to the following controversial verse.

Matthew 7:1-2 "Do not judge so that you will not be judged. "For in the way you judge, you will be judged; and by your standard of measure, it will be measured to you."

This is the most often quoted verse when dealing with the subject of judging. In addition, it is usually quoted with the wrong meaning. Anytime a person makes a judgment with regard to another person, this verse is thrown out there to impugn the one who made the judgment.

In order to put this in perspective let us set up the scene. There is a difference between Jesus' communication to the crowds and to His students. To His students, He would speak words of training and instruction, such as in the case here. This was an instruction to His disciples. Next, let us add some context to get an understanding.

Matthew 7:3-5 "Why do you look at the speck that is in your brother's eye, but do not notice the log that is in your own eye? Or how can you say to your brother, 'Let me take the speck out of your eye,' and behold, the log is in your own eye? 'You hypocrite, first take the log out of your own eye, and then you will see clearly to take the speck out of your brother's eye."

Now we see what Jesus is speaking about. The context is inter-disciple relationships. Why would Jesus tell his disciples not to judge when telling them that they would be judges over the twelve tribes of Israel? Could it be that they are in training and need some maturity to become righteous judges?

Also, Jesus is not telling them not to judge, but not to judge in an unrighteous way; otherwise, He would not have said first get the log out of your eye then you will see clearly to remove the speck in your brother's eye. So, when people quote that verse as a moratorium against judging they misinterpret its meaning.

Jesus is training disciples to become bishops, not apostles. Apostles were who they were from birth, whereas bishops and elders were what they were to become. Their calling as apostles was a revelation of who God created them to be. God had wove into their spirit all the necessary components and gifts to function perfectly as apostles. That being said, to be a judge or bishop, they would need training.

Often the minister in training thinks that he or she is being trained to be a prophet, apostle, teacher, evangelist, or pastor. There are some components of training that will help develop those gifts, as well as guidelines in operating in their call. However, the bulk of training will develop the leader and that leader will be an elder who can become a bishop.

> **Jeremiah 1:5** *"Before I formed you in the womb I knew you, And before you were born I consecrated you; I have appointed you a prophet to the nations."*

Jeremiah was called from the womb to be a prophet. He did not have to become a prophet, but was ordained as one by his Maker.

Summation

- Calling or ministry is who we are and it is identified as apostle, prophet, pastor, teacher, or evangelist.
- Elder is a certain level of maturity manifest in character, knowledge, gift operation, and relationships.

- Bishop or judge is an office of oversight that results in the church being shepherded.

Before we get into the callings, we need to address the role of women in ministry. That is the subject of the next chapter.

He Called Her "Woman"

Chapter Four

Part One: God's Image

> *Genesis 1:26-27 Then God said, "Let Us make*
> *man in Our image, according to Our likeness; and*
> *let them rule over the fish of the sea and over the*
> *birds of the sky and over the cattle and over all the*
> *earth, and over every creeping thing that creeps on*
> *the earth." God created man in His own image, in*
> *the image of God He created him; male and female*
> *He created them.*

To begin this lesson we need to understand the creation of man and woman so we can get a complete picture of the role they have in contrast and in likeness to one another. In the Scripture above, we need to point out a number of things in order to make sense of what is said.

"Let Us make man in Our image according to Our likeness..." is one phrase where we find the idea of the Trinity. In this phrase, God does not speak of Himself in the singular; God uses the plural form of personal pronouns to describe His nature. Still, we know that God is One.

That should be clear enough to you so that we can move forward. For the sake of this chapter, we don't necessarily need to understand the concept of the Trinity; we just need to understand that God is One and at times refers to Himself in the plural form.

Image

Now we move to the next stage of understanding. To do that, let's ask the question: *"What does it mean to be created in the 'image' of God?"* To answer that, we will look to the Hebrew word used for "image."

DEFINITION

*6754 [tselem /tseh·lem/] n m. From an unused root meaning **to shade**; 1 image. 1a images (of tumours, mice, heathen gods). 1b image, likeness (of resemblance). 1c mere, empty, image, semblance (fig.).*[9]

So the real meaning of "image" is "shadow." The shadow of something is never the thing itself. The idea that we are gods because we are created in the image of God is nonsensical. The shadow of a thing is not the thing itself, but rather just an outline or a vague copy of the original. This means that when God created man, He created a shadow or outline of Himself.

If God refers to Himself in the plural form and God created man in His shadow, then would it not be likely that man would be referred to in the plural as well? Indeed! If you were to look at a photograph of yourself, you would see only a shadow of yourself or a likeness of yourself. That photograph would not be you, but it would have your likeness. But if you referred to yourself in the photo you would say something like, *"That's me right there."* It would follow that when God looks at His image (us) He would use language like, *"That's Us right*

---

[9]Strong, J. 1996. *Enhanced Strong's Lexicon.* Woodside Bible Fellowship: Ontario.

there." The Bible says that God is not a man (Numbers 23:19). The Bible also says that God is spirit (John 4:24). As a spirit, God does not possess a body or flesh.

The reason this is important is that if God is not physical, yet He made us physical beings, then the image that God is speaking of is not that we have physical appearance like Him because He does not possess a physical image. In fact, we find that the Apostle Paul refers to the body as the temple of God. That means that the body would be a likeness of the temple of God rather than the image of God.

The image is something about God that was transposed into our creation, but it is not the way we look. Our likeness of God is not to be a god, so the idea of looking like God or being God is eliminated in the idea of the image of God. What we are left with is a shadow of the nature of God. What we mean by nature is the framework of God or the structure of God, His likeness.

Let's go back to the shadow. A shadow is the outline of the original. If you see a shadow of a building, you can make out the outline of the building - not the essence of it, but the outline of it, its construction, if you will. Yet God is not physical; He is spirit, so we are not speaking of the physical but the spiritual. God is also three in one. That means that we are three in one as well. If God then refers to Himself in the plural form, does it not follow that He will create us in such a way that we refer to us in the plural also?

"Male and female created He them...." This is a very significant phrase. To understand this we need to differentiate between some words. The word "created" is the Hebrew *bara [baw-raw]* and it simply means "to create." It is the same word used in the first verse of Genesis when God said, *"In the beginning God **created** the heavens and the earth."* This means that both

Adam and Eve were **created**. Remember this because it is extremely important.

DEFINITION

1254 [bara' /baw·raw/] v. A primitive root; 1 to create, shape, form. 1a (Qal) to shape, fashion, create (always with God as subject). 1a1 of heaven and earth. 1a2 of individual man. 1a3 of new conditions and circumstances. 1a4 of transformations.[10]

When we look at the account of Eve becoming a physical being, a different Hebrew word is employed.

*Genesis 2:21-22 So the Lord God caused a deep sleep to fall upon the man, and he slept; then He took one of his ribs and closed up the flesh at that place. The Lord God **fashioned** into a woman the rib which He had taken from the man, and brought her to the man.*

DEFINITION

1129 [banah /baw·naw/] v. A primitive root; 1 to build, rebuild, establish, cause to continue.[11]

God **built** Eve into a physical woman. Since the word "create" is not used here in the making of woman, we must conclude that woman already existed before this event happened.

---

[10]Strong, J. 1996. *Enhanced Strong's Lexicon.* Woodside Bible Fellowship: Ontario.

[11]Strong, J. 1996. *Enhanced Strong's Lexicon.* Woodside Bible Fellowship: Ontario.

This means that woman would have already been created, but she was not yet built into a physical form. This begs the question, *"If the woman was already created, where was she?"* It goes back to the Scripture where God said, *"Male and female created He them...."* Was Adam in the form of both male and female? Not in a physical sense but in a spiritual one? Is that why God referred to Adam as "them" just as He refers to Himself as "Us."

> **Genesis 5:2 (KJV)** *Male and female created he* **them**; *and blessed* **them**, *and* **called their name Adam, in the day** *when they were created.*

Why does the Bible say that God called "their" name "Adam?" The idea here cannot be lost. God called Adam a "their." This is just another proof that God created man and woman that were housed in one physical body. Notice also the phrase "in the day when they were created." They were created in the same day.

One of the reasons this is important is that there are those who say that woman was not created and that only man was created and woman was formed from man; then they use this as a reason to suppress the role of women in the Kingdom of God.

> **Genesis 1:28** *God blessed* **them**; *and God said to* **them**, *"Be fruitful and multiply, and fill the earth, and subdue it; and rule over the fish of the sea and over the birds of the sky and over every living thing that moves on the earth."*

Again, God is here referring only to Adam as "them." How do we know this? Eve has not been taken out of Adam yet. Some have said that chapters one and two of Genesis are parallel accounts of the creation. The reason they think this is because chapter two goes into a more detailed account of the creation of man. Nonetheless, there are some things that lead us to believe that the author is only reiterating at times the creation in chapter one.

> *Genesis 1:29-31 Then God said, "Behold, I have given you every plant yielding seed that is on the surface of all the earth, and every tree which has fruit yielding seed; it shall be food for you; and to every beast of the earth and to every bird of the sky and to every thing that moves on the earth which has life, I have given every green plant for food"; and it was so. God saw all that He had made, and behold, it was very good. And there was evening and there was morning, the sixth day.*

> *Genesis 2:15-17 Then the Lord God took the man and put him into the garden of Eden to cultivate it and keep it. The Lord God commanded the man, saying, "From any tree of the garden you may eat freely; but from the tree of the knowledge of good and evil you shall not eat, for in the day that you eat from it you will surely die."*

In the first section of Scripture quoted here, God is still talking to only Adam as "them." This agrees with the second set that shows God said this to Adam before Eve was formed. If God in chapter one said He created them male and female and the next verse says He said to them that you will have dominion and you can eat the plants for food, and then we find in the next section that God is giving Adam instruction about what he can eat, we are left with the conclusion that Eve is still inside Adam. It isn't until Genesis 2:21-22 that Eve is formed out of the side of Adam.

All of these things support the idea that God created in Adam both man and woman. **In that quintessence they were the image of God and Adam was referred to as "them," yet they**

were one flesh. When God separated Eve from Adam, He no longer refers to Adam as "them" nor to Eve as "them." But notice a very important phrase.

> **Genesis 2:24** *For this reason a man shall leave his father and his mother, and be joined to his wife; and* ***they shall become one flesh.***

We see that it is only when a man and woman come together that they are referred to as "they" and one flesh. **This means that the image of God is completed again when men and women come together in marriage.** (By the way, this is the verse that instituted marriage for the first time. It is instituted by God, not by man.)

We begin to get an understanding of the importance of the definition of marriage. It is not man with man or woman with woman for that would pollute the picture of the image of God. This is why God said that a man shall not lie with a man like a woman for it is an abomination (Romans 1:26-28).

God created Adam in His image and refers to Adam as "them." In this state, Adam is man, woman, and flesh, yet they are one. God is Father, Word (Son), and Holy Spirit, but they are One. Adam is the image of God. Now God deems it necessary to split Adam into two physical beings. Thus Eve is taken from Adam's side, from Adam's DNA. It is at this point that God says *"For this reason a man shall leave his father and mother and be joined to his wife; and they shall become one flesh."* Through marriage the image of God is again joined together into one flesh.

With this understanding in mind, we get the idea that woman is a part of the image of God, man is another part of the image of God, and the body is the final part of the image of God. That means that we should treat each other and our bodies with respect to the image of God. At this time I want to bring you four thousand years into the future from the point of creation. God is now on earth as a man…His name is Jesus, and what He says has great import to our understanding.

> **Mark 10:2-9** *Some Pharisees came up to Jesus, testing Him, and began to question Him whether it was lawful for a man to divorce a wife. And He answered and said to them, "What did Moses command you?" They said, "Moses permitted a man to write a certificate of divorce and send her away."*
>
> *But Jesus said to them, "Because of your hardness of heart he wrote you this commandment. "But from the beginning of creation, God made them male and female. "**For this reason** a man shall leave his father and mother, and the two shall become one flesh; so they are no longer two, but one flesh. "What therefore God has joined together, let no man separate."*

"For what reason…?" What was Jesus referring to? He was referring to the fact that God created Adam as one person, both male and female, then after separating them, calls them to come back together to be joined again and re-complete the image of God. Remember that God is the one who caused the separation in Genesis 2:22-23; furthermore, in verse 24 God is the One who joins them back together. What God is saying is that man could not separate Adam, and when man and woman come together to make one again, the Adam, or man, has no right to separate the two. Jesus is quoting from Genesis 2:23-24, so now would be a good time to look at verse 23.

Genesis 2:23 The man [120] said [559], "This [2088] is now [6471] bone [6106] of my bones [6106], And flesh [1320] of my flesh [1320]; She shall be called [7121] Woman [802], Because [3588] she was taken [3947] out of Man [376]."

I included the Strong's Concordance numbers so you can easily look them up yourself and to show you the contrast. There are two places in this verse where the word "man" is used. Notice, though, that there are two different numbers that correspond to two different words. In the first instance it is "Adam" and in the second it is *iysh (eesh)*. Remember that the term "Adam" is used to include both male and female.

For the first time we have a different Hebrew word used, *iysh,* which refers solely to the male gender; then we have introduced for the second time the word *ishshah (eesh-shaw),* to refer to the female gender. The first time it is used is in verse 22 when it says that God fashioned the rib into a *woman (ishshah.)*

This is significant in light of what we've already learned. From here on the Bible uses the term "Adam" as inclusive of both men and women, and it is sometimes rendered mankind. The Bible uses the word *iysh* to refer to the male gender and *ishshah* to refer to the female gender. When an *iysh* and an *ishshah* come together in marriage, together they become Adam and complete again the image of God. Let's look at some evidence to make this point clear.

Genesis 9:6 "Whoever sheds man's blood, By man his blood shall be shed, For in the image of God He made man.

The word "man" or "man's" is the Hebrew "Adam." If this referred to the male gender only, then the murder of women would be allowed. Of course, we know this is not the case. Thus, the word "Adam" is usually used in the sense of both male and female.

Idolatry & Adultery

> *Exodus 32:20 He took the calf which they had made and burned it with fire, and ground it to powder, and scattered it over the surface of the water and made the sons of Israel drink it.*

This verse is the response Moses had when he came down the mountain and found that the nation of Israel had fallen into idolatry. He took the idol and burned it with fire. Then, after grinding it to powder, he scattered the powder over the surface of the water and made those who had committed idolatry drink the water.

> *Numbers 5:17 and the priest shall take holy water in an earthenware vessel; and he shall take some of the dust that is on the floor of the tabernacle and put it into the water.*

> *Numbers 5:24 'Then he shall make the woman drink the water of bitterness that brings a curse, so that the water which brings a curse will go into her and cause bitterness.*

The purpose of contrasting these two sections of Scripture is to show that idolatry has some of the same punishments as adultery. The reason becomes clear when we understand the image of God. God is a unity of one. When a man or woman goes outside the marriage and commits adultery, it is not just a violation of the union, but it is a violation of the image of God. The person who commits adultery makes the image of God into something that He is not, thus the idea of idolatry is introduced. God is not divided. He is the holy One. He is in perfect unity.

> **Ezekiel 6:9** *"Then those of you who escape will remember Me among the nations to which they will be carried captive, how I have been hurt by their adulterous hearts which turned away from Me, and by their eyes which **played the harlot after their idols**; and they will loathe themselves in their own sight for the evils which they have committed, for all their abominations."*

> **Ezekiel 23:37** *"For they have committed adultery, and blood is on their hands. Thus they have committed adultery with their idols and even caused their sons, whom they bore to Me, to pass through the fire to them as food."*

In these Scriptures we see that God sees idolatry as adultery. It originates from a heart that is NOT devoted to the image of God. Remember what Jesus said about divorce? First, it is only allowed in the case of adultery. Second, it was only allowed because of the hardness of their hearts. Adultery starts in the heart of a person. It is having a hard heart; it is a heart that does not care about one's spouse, but is only devoted to self and self-satisfaction.

> *"QUOTE"*

> *"Returning to Genesis 1:27, there is another p'shat reading that I believe supports the idea of the Trinity. The words of this verse are: '...in the image of God he created him; male and female he created them.' Always before when I read this text, I gave the 'male and female' portion little*

thought, because it seemed obvious God created both men and women. But why state the obvious?

At Chever Torah, as we study the scriptural idea that Adam and Eve were 'one flesh,' the following concept is presented: 'When a soul is sent down from Heaven, it is a combined male and female soul.'

--Zohar, iii, 43b

When I learned about this theory, suddenly the notion that man was created in God's image as both male and female takes on a new level of meaning, and I glimpse an important possibility in the verse that says he made us male and female in his image. Could it be phrased in that way because the creation of men and women is meant to be a reflection of the divine plurality?

What if men, women, and the third thing we become when joined together— the 'one flesh'– are somehow meant to be an earthly image and likeness of the three persons of God?

*This has important ramifications not only in my understanding of God's nature, but also in terms of marriage. It explains why sexual sin is dealt with so severely in the Torah. **Adultery equals Idolatry.*** " [12]

---

[12] *-- "The Gospel According to Moses" By Athol Dickson*

Some of the rebuttals I have received from others when they hear this teaching is that man was created first. Let's take a look at that.

> ***1 Timothy 2:13*** *For it was Adam who was first created, and then Eve.*

We need to take a look at the original language to get to the true meaning of the word "create." The Greek word is *plasso* and its meaning is "to form." It does not correspond to the word for create which is the Greek word *ktizo*. If we look into how the word *plasso* is used in the Septuagint we will see that this word corresponds to the Hebrew word used in the formation of Adam's body.

> ***Genesis 2:7*** *Then the LORD God formed man of dust from the ground, and breathed into his nostrils the breath of life; and man became a living being.*

The Hebrew word "formed" is *yatsar* and it means "to form." It is literally a potter. What is interesting here is that the word used for the formation of Eve's body is not the same word used for Adam's. The word used for Adam's body does not have the sense of causing to continue as Eve's does. So the theory remains intact.

It is my purpose for this that men and women will see themselves as a part of the image of God's triune nature. In doing so we will all give greater import to the part that women play in the Kingdom of God. If men withhold positions from women in the Church, they are suppressing the image of God from being manifest through us…humanity…the Adam.

Part 2: Women in Leadership

When we begin to talk about women in leadership, we want to include leadership in both the Church and the world. When speaking of women in leadership positions, there has long been a move to suppress women from these positions. A person need only think for a moment, and one can throw out some names of women who led in such a way that they brought honor to their countries. You may think of Golda Meir from Israel, Margaret Thatcher from Great Brittan, or Rosa Parks, whose quiet refusal to submit to the racist voices any longer was able to bring positive change to the United States. There are scores of other examples from the political realm to the sacred realm.

There are many voices calling for the opening of positions in the political and sacred arenas long held by men to become available to women. What I want to focus on is the realm of the sacred. Women have been told for centuries that they are not allowed to hold positions of authority in the Church. People have many and varied reasons for thinking this way, and I want to take a close look at these reasons to see if what people are saying is true.

If these voices in the Church that are opposed to women in leadership positions are right and articulate the will of God, then I want to come into agreement with that. In other words, **I am not on a vendetta to put women in leadership.** My goal is to seek the truth and will of God and follow it. If God prohibits women in leadership, then I should be in agreement with God. On the other hand, if God has not prohibited women from being in leadership, then we need to come into agreement with that and allow women to take their place according to the will of God.

Opposing Arguments

Anytime I attempt to bring light to a controversial subject, I always like to start by studying the arguments connected with it. To be fair, I have only studied the arguments that seek to keep women **out of** positions of leadership. Again, my goal is to find the truth. Why is that being fair? I believe it is fair because in studying the Word of God, I do not see God suppressing women in the same scope and manner as these men have. Therefore, to balance the argument, I only studied those positions that seek to keep women out of these places of leadership.

The Curse

The argument always starts with the curse placed on women by God in the Garden of Eden. Let's take a look at it.

> **Genesis 3:16** *To the woman He said, "I will greatly multiply Your pain in childbirth, In pain you will bring forth children; Yet your desire will be for your husband, And he will rule over you."*

Of course, the section we are interested in is the last part of this verse. This section is quoted to voice opposition to women in leadership positions. It is argued that because man is to rule over woman that women should never be placed in a position of authority over man in government, business, church, etc. We need to dissect this and see what it is that God is actually saying. First, we need to determine something important from the outset. Either:

- All men are in authority over all women and, therefore,
  - Any man is in authority over all women or

- Husbands are in authority **only** over their wives.

From reading this text, it is clear that it cannot be stated that all men have authority over all women. **This curse is only confined to marriage.** That is the only conclusion we can make. When we look at the word for "husband" in Hebrew, it is *iysh*. As we learned in Part I of this lesson, *iysh* is a word to distinguish the male gender. Some will argue that since this word is used to distinguish the male gender, it supports their argument that all men have authority over all women. All we need to do, though, is find another place this word is used to describe a woman's husband and, at the very least, we have neutralized that argument.

What we find is that it is used, not just once or twice, but several times to describe a woman's husband. Look up the following references and you will find that every place the word *"husband"* is rendered in English, the Hebrew is *iysh*. You can see this throughout Numbers chapter 30; Judges 13:6,9,10; 14:15; 19:3; 20:4; and Ruth 1:3,5,9,11,12; 2:1,11.

These are only a few of the passages that demonstrate this point. It becomes abundantly clear that the Hebrew word *iysh* is used to distinguish the male gender and a woman's husband. If that were the only evidence we had, it would be enough to at least neutralize the argument that all men have authority over all women. Even so, that is not all the evidence that we have. Let's take a look at some more.

> **Ephesians 5:22** *Wives, **be subject to your own husbands**, as to the Lord.*

> **Colossians 3:18** *Wives, be subject to your husbands, as is fitting in the Lord.*

> **Titus 2:4-5** *so that they may encourage the young women to love their husbands, to love their children, to be sensible, pure, workers at home,*

*kind, **being subject to their own husbands**, so that the word of God will not be dishonored.*

***1 Peter 3:1** In the same way, **you wives, be submissive to your own husbands** so that even if any of them are disobedient to the word, they may be won without a word by the behavior of their wives,*

It becomes obvious that God did not give all males authority over all females. If He had would not the term "women be subject to all men" be used? Every time the words "wife" and "submit" are used together, it is always in reference to the husband only. That being said, you wives might be a bit perturbed to find out that your husbands are to be the object of your submission. We still only have half of the story.

***Ephesians 5:25** Husbands, love your wives, just as Christ also loved the church and gave Himself up for her...*

Only when we put the two halves together do we get a picture of the whole. Yes, wives are to be subject to their husbands; however, husbands are to love their wives as Christ loved the Church and gave Himself for her. We are the Church; we are the Bride of Christ. Jesus speaks of us ruling and reigning with Him. Not only is that a position of authority, but who did Jesus put in charge of His affairs on earth? Yes, it is the Church, the Bride.

Therefore, husbands, if your wife is called of God to hold a place of authority in the Church and you forbid it; you do not love your wife as Christ loved the Church. If you love your wife and you love God, you will encourage your wife to take her place according to the will of God. She is just as important to the image of God as you are. There is much more evidence concerning this, but I think this should suffice to move to the next argument.

Silence in the Church

> *1 Corinthians 14:34-35 The women are to keep silent in the churches; for they are not permitted to speak, but are to subject themselves, just as the Law also says. If they desire to learn anything, let them ask their own husbands at home; for it is improper for a woman to speak in church.*

This is the next argument concerning women holding authority or even speaking or teaching in the Church. On the surface this appears to be saying that women are not allowed to speak in church. I would argue that churches that refuse to let women teach in the Church do not follow this verse for they would have to silence them completely.

If you are going to use this as an evidence to keep women from positions in church, then by all means follow it to the letter. The fact that most only use it to suppress but do not actually implement it shows us how disingenuous this doctrine is.

Again, we first have to see if this applies to all women or does it just apply to wives as in the first argument. In light of verse thirty-five, it is quite clear that Paul is speaking only to wives.

The second objection that I have is if **women or wives** are not to speak in the Church, then the rest of Scripture will have to agree with this statement. Doing a little investigating, we find that God has gifted women to speak in the congregation of saints.

> *Acts 2:17-18 'And it shall be in the last days,' God says, 'That I will pour forth of My Spirit on all mankind; And your sons and your **daughters shall**

*prophesy, And your young men shall see visions, And your old men shall dream dreams; Even on My bondslaves, **both men and women**, I will in those days pour forth of My Spirit And they shall prophesy.'*

Once more, it becomes obvious that if God gives a gift of prophecy to a woman that He expects her to use it. How can she use it unless she speaks in the Church those things God is giving her to say? The Apostle Paul speaks about the gift of prophecy as edifying, or building up the Church. If this is so and women are to prophecy, then it is clearly obvious that God intends them to do so in the Church.

> **Luke 2:36** *And there was a prophetess, Anna the daughter of Phanuel, of the tribe of Asher. She was advanced in years and had lived with her husband seven years after her marriage...*

> **Acts 21:8-9** *On the next day we left and came to Caesarea, and entering the house of Philip the evangelist, who was one of the seven, we stayed with him. Now this man had four virgin daughters who were prophetesses.*

If God has given the office of prophet to a woman, according to Ephesians 4:11, she is supposed to equip the saints to do the work of God. **How can she teach and equip the saints if she is not allowed to speak in the Church?** I realize that these two examples are of women who are not married; however, do they lose their gifts and calling once they get married? The Bible tells us that the gifts and call of God are given without revocation (Romans 11:29). That means once God calls a person and gives them gifts, He will not take them back.

Once the woman is married to her husband and her husband refuses to allow her to preach or teach, then she must comply, but the responsibility for completing her call has now fallen upon her husband since he is her head. He must give an account to God for his decision. Not only this, but by forbidding her from fulfilling her call he is also forbidding God from working through her and again he obviously does not love his wife as Christ loves the Church and gave Himself for her.

What, then, could Paul be speaking of when he made the statement that women are to be silent in the Church? The clue to what he was really trying to say is found in 1 Corinthians 14:35 where he makes the statement that the wives are to ask their husbands at home. If we take this statement and place it in the context of chapter fourteen and look at some peculiarities of the culture of that time period, then we can begin to understand what Paul was saying.

First, we will determine the context. It must be noted that the Apostle Paul is answering some questions that were written to him by the Corinthian church. Not having those questions puts us at a disadvantage in understanding. Nevertheless, we can deduce certain things by looking at Paul's answers. In chapter fourteen, Paul is dealing with confusion and disorder in the church.

✓ In the first part of this chapter Paul is dealing with the confusion that had arisen because of the people speaking in tongues in the church. Unbelievers would come in and would be confused hearing all of the chatter as a result of many people speaking in tongues at the same time.

✓ Then, Paul moves from this to prophecy. The church was allowing several prophets to prophecy at the same time. Again, this brought disorder and confusion. Thus, Paul commanded all the prophets to prophecy one at a time so that all could hear and be blessed.

✓ Following this issue, Paul commands women to keep silent in the church.

It becomes obvious to us when we consider the context that Paul is addressing the problems that were bringing disorder in the church. What does this issue of wives speaking in church have to do with confusion? To that we must address the culture of the time.

"QUOTE"

The last point is decisive and shows that Sha'ul is answering a question (7:1) the Corinthians asked about wives' discussing with their husbands what is being said while it is being said. This would disturb decorum even if the wife were sitting next to her husband; but if the universal Jewish practice of the time (and of Orthodox congregations today) was followed, wherein women and men are seated separately in the synagogue, it would obviously be intolerable to have wives and husbands yelling at each other across the mchitzah (dividing wall). Sha'ul places his instruction precisely here in the letter because it is here that he is dealing with matters of decorum and public order in congregational meetings; his advice seems curt and abrupt only if one ignores that he has already discussed the applicable general principles and that (by my assumption) his questioners are already familiar with the context of the problem, since they brought it up in the first place. If we could not supply such a framework for these verses, we might have to conclude, as some do, that Sha'ul demeans women[13]

When we understand that women were on one side and men on the other with a dividing wall between them, we begin to understand what Paul means. Notice that Paul was not addressing women in general, but only wives. This is so because in that culture when the wives did not understand something they were to ask their husbands. Then the husband would answer or ask the question himself. This would result in wives shouting to their husbands asking them questions about the things they were hearing. Thus, we understand the statement Paul makes in verse 35 telling the wives to ask their husbands at home so that the church would not be out of order.

Paul did not deal with whether that cultural practice was correct; rather his concern was for order in the church. Instead, he appeals to the law *(...they are to subject themselves as the Law says.)* to tell the wives that they are to yield themselves to their husbands, so they need to ask them at home rather than disrupting the church.

Authority in the Church

*1 **Timothy 2:11-15** A woman must quietly receive instruction with entire submissiveness. But I do not allow a woman to teach or exercise authority over a man, but to remain quiet. For it was Adam who was first created, and then Eve. And it was not Adam*

---

[13]Stern, D. H. 1992. *Jewish New Testament Commentary: A companion volume to the Jewish New Testament.* Includes index. (1st ed.) . Jewish New Testament Publications: Clarksville, Md.

who was deceived, but the woman being deceived,
fell into transgression. But women will be preserved
through the bearing of children if they continue in
faith and love and sanctity with self-restraint.

This is one of the most quoted sections in the Bible concerning women in leadership positions. I think it important to point out some things in order that we do not get off track.

- ✓ It is fair to say that God does not break His own order or His own commands in order to get something done.

- ✓ Having said that, if God has commanded that women in general are not to have authority over any man, then we have a problem if...

- ✓ we find Biblically just one instance of a woman being in authority over man by the will of God. If that is the case then we are left with the conclusion that either God is breaking His own order and law or we are misunderstanding the Scripture in Timothy.

Let me simplify this a bit. God is the One Who said, *"Thou shalt not steal."* Is there any situation where God would encourage one to steal? If there is, then God ceases to be God for the Bible says that God cannot lie. That is the great thing about absolute nature. We always know that it is wrong for us to steal. The same goes for women in leadership. As a result, I present the example of Deborah.

Deborah

*Judges 4:4-5 Now Deborah, a **prophetess**, the **wife** of Lappidoth, was judging Israel at that time. She used to sit under the palm tree of Deborah between*

Ramah and Bethel in the hill country of Ephraim;
and the sons of Israel came up to her for judgment.

Here we have a woman, who is also married by the way, sitting in judgment over the nation of Israel. **At this time she is the highest authority in Israel.** Notice that the men **come to her** for judgment. If you read the whole story of Deborah you will find that Deborah **commanded the commander** of the armies of Israel to go to war. This commander said he would only go if Deborah went with him.

To that request she agreed to go and she told the commander that he would win the war, but that the glory of the victory would go to a woman. As they went to war, they defeated the opposing army and they began a pursuit of the commander of that army. The commander of the opposing army came to a camp and was brought into a tent so that he could rest. As he slept, a woman took a tent peg and drove it through his head. Thus a woman received the glory for victory just as Deborah prophesied.

I have heard many people say that Deborah was the leader at this time only because there were no men up to the task. Again, that argument presupposes that God violates His own divine order. If God does not permit a woman or a wife to be in leadership, then He violated His own command. Are we to believe that God is so weak that He could not raise up a man so He had to violate His own command? That is absurd. The only conclusion that we can come to is that God **did not violate** His own command. **This suggests that God is NOT opposed to women in leadership.**

✓ God had to give Deborah the gift of prophecy to operate in the office of prophet. This was the gifting that allowed her to operate as a judge in Israel.

✓ From this we must conclude that Deborah was operating in accordance with the will of God for her life. Not only this, but…

✓ Deborah had a husband who was willing to let her fulfill the position to which God had called her. He recognized his wife's gifting and calling and was willing to assist her even if it meant that he was in the background. As such, he was allowing the will of God to be accomplished through his wife.

✓ That is the pattern God wants us to repeat.

If we go back and revisit the Scripture in Timothy, we can see that God **is not** forbidding a woman from being in leadership; rather, Paul is admonishing women **not to seek to be in authority over their husbands.** Was Lappidoth still in authority over Deborah while she was a judge? Of course he was. That is the order God has given to us, but Lappidoth was able to see that God had called his wife, and he allowed it to take place according to the will of God.

Again, this can only be looked at from the confines of marriage. Paul brings in Adam and Eve as reasons for his argument. Paul reiterated that God had established authority in the marriage relationship. If we don't understand what we learned from the first part of this lesson about woman being a part of the image of God, then we get the wrong idea of the order of marriage.

Marriage was not meant to be an unequal coupling. Husbands need to see their wives as equals, and wives need to see their husbands as equals. **The positions are irrelevant to value.** Notice how Jesus yields Himself to the Father. He is equal with the Father, but He steps back and lets the Father lead. If we are to mimic the image of God in our relationship of marriage, it only makes sense that one will yield to the other.

We have already dealt with the eleventh verse of I Timothy. In verse twelve, Paul is not saying that all women are under the authority of men; rather, he is saying that only the husband is to have authority in the relationship of marriage. We know this because there are Biblical examples of women in leadership positions. All Paul is trying to do here is to keep the correct order of marriage, thus preserving the image of God. Paul goes back to Genesis to validate his argument.

The last verse in this section need not be controversial. First, we have to remember that Paul is in Genesis. He is referring to the curse put on women. That curse is the pain of child bearing and that of having husbands who rule over them. Paul is appealing to women to accept God's curse. Women will be preserved through the pain of childbirth if they will keep faith. I could also add to this that men will be preserved through the sweat of his brow if they will keep faith.

This concludes the section on opposing arguments. It should be clear to you that **not all men have authority over all women.** It is only within the confines of marriage that a husband has authority over his wife. This means that a woman who is single can function in the Church just as a man. Remember, the Greek word used for wife and woman is the same, and the Greek word used for husband and man is the same. We have to distinguish one from the other by the context.

Divine Order

We are now going to look at another section of Scripture that is used to suppress women. I did not include it in the previous section because it also shows the divine order of creation, so I saved it for this section.

> *1 Corinthians 11:3 But I want you to understand that Christ is the head of every man, and the man is the head of a woman, and God is the head of Christ.*

Before we look at the order I want you to notice that the word "every" is used with regard to Christ being head over every man, however, notice that when it comes to man he is only head of "a" woman. This reiterates that not every man is the head of every woman. In this one verse Paul lays out the divine order. In this one verse we learn that Christ is in subjection, man is in subjection, and woman is in subjection.

- ✓ God is the head of Christ.
- ✓ Christ is the head of man.
- ✓ Man is the head of woman.

Now that we have established this, we cannot lose sight of the idea of Christ being in subjection to the Father. This is the model we are to follow. That is:

- ✓ As a man, I am to submit myself to Christ as Christ submitted Himself to God.
- ✓ As a woman, you are to submit yourself to your husband as Christ submitted Himself to God.

Christ is the model of submission. **He does not see submission as demeaning**. We need to quit looking at "submission" as a dirty word. Both men and women are to submit. This is the divine order of creation. Remember, however, this is only within the confines of marriage for the woman. Outside of marriage we are all to submit to Christ. Remember what the word "submit" means? It means to yield to another. Every time you slow down while driving your car to allow another car to merge into traffic, you just submitted to the other car. It was an act of your free-will and not compulsion from the person driving the other car. It did not demean you, reduce your value, or make you subhuman.

> ***1 Corinthians 11:4-6*** *Every man who has something on his head while praying or prophesying disgraces his head. But every woman who has her head uncovered while praying or prophesying disgraces her head, for she is one and the same as the woman whose head is shaved. For if a woman does not cover her head, let her also have her hair cut off; but if it is disgraceful for a woman to have her hair cut off or her head shaved, let her cover her head.*

Before we discuss this section we need to reveal Paul's context. Look at how he starts this chapter.

> ***1 Corinthians 11:1-2*** *Be imitators of me, just as I also am of Christ. Now I praise you because you remember me in everything and hold firmly to the traditions, just as I delivered them to you.*

It is important to understand that Paul uses the word "traditions" before he embarks upon this information about head coverings. Traditions are diverse in different cultures. If we are not to offend cultures, then we need to respect their traditions in order that we do not bring a reproach to Christ. It is only when those traditions are opposed to God and His Word that we are to ignore them. As Jesus Himself said, *"...your traditions of men make the Word of God of no effect"* (Mark 7:13). Therefore, when dealing with traditions, we need to be careful not to transfer traditions of another culture into our culture as a commandment of God.

The head covering that is talked about here is not a hat but a veil. The idea is this: Since the head of man is Christ, when man is praying or prophesying, he is doing so by direction of his Head, which is Christ. Although, when a woman who is married is prophesying she is also under the direction of Christ, but she has an authority that is between her and Christ. Wearing the veil reveals that she has an authority between her and the One in Whose name she is prophesying.

This is why it is a shame for a man to wear a veil while praying or prophesying, because that would suggest another is in authority between him and Christ and would thus pollute the divine order of authority. On the contrary, if the woman did not wear the veil while praying or prophesying, she would be ignoring the authority of her husband and this, too, would pollute the divine order of creation. Everyone of that culture understood these things and, if this protocol was violated, it would bring offence to the people and reproach to Christ. However, in our society, the wearing of a veil would produce the opposite effect. If we followed these traditions today, people would look at Christians as an oppressive society and thus bring a reproach to Christ.

"QUOTE"

A cover for the face; a disguise. From the earliest times it has been a sign of chastity and decency in married women to cover their faces with veils in the presence of strangers. This custom is still in vogue in the Orient. The putting on of the veil marked the transition from girlhood to womanhood. Rebekah, the bride, covered herself with a veil on meeting Isaac, the groom (Gen. xxiv. 65). A widow did not wear a veil (ib. xxxviii. 19). The custom of dressing the virgin bride with a veil is mentioned in the Mishnah; covered with a veil ("hinuma") and seated on a litter, she was carried in the wedding-procession from her father's house to the nuptial ceremony (Ket. ii. 1). In modern times the bride is "covered" with a veil in her chamber in the presence of the groom, just before they are led under the canopy. In some countries the groom, and in others the rabbi, performs the ceremony of covering the bride. [14]

---

1 Corinthians 11:6 For if a woman does not cover her head, let her also have her hair cut off; but if it is disgraceful for a woman to have her hair cut off or her head shaved, let her cover her head.

The idea of this verse is that if a wife of that culture did not want to cover the front of her head, let the back of her head be exposed as well. This shows us the extent of offence this brought upon someone of this culture. Again, it must be reiterated that we are talking only about wives.

1 Corinthians 11:7-10 For a man ought not to have his head covered, since he is the image and glory of God; but the woman is the glory of man. For man does not originate from woman, but woman from man; for indeed man was not created for the woman's sake, but woman for the man's sake. Therefore the woman ought to have a symbol of authority on her head, because of the angels.

---

[14] -- *Jewish Encyclopedia*

Paul reveals the reasoning behind the head covering or veil. Since Eve was made for Adam's sake, she is to have a symbol of authority on her head. It is vital that you realize that woman existed inside of Adam before she was removed, just as Christ was in perfect unity with the Godhead before He was extracted and took on the form of flesh. This is why He put Himself in subjection to the Father. He came from the Father. Woman is the picture of Christ. She came from the man. This is why in the marriage there must be the retention of the image of God.

All this has to do with position. We see this all the time in the Body of Christ. People are created and placed in a position within the Body. We should not try to vie for another's position but rather be pleased to take our place as God has given it. It has nothing to do with the value or ability that a person has. God deems us all as valuable. Too much emphasis has been placed on the position and not enough emphasis has been placed on the individual's value.

Is Jesus any less valuable because He has yielded or submitted to the Father? Is He less talented or less important? Of course not! Therefore, wives are not less valuable because of their position to their husbands. Both sexes should see one another as part of the image of God, focusing not on each other's position to one another. It is only God's divine order, and nothing more should be made of it. Also I hesitate to keep reminding you of this, but we are only talking about the relationship between husband and wife. It is easy to lose sight of that when dealing with the wording of these Scriptures.

Examples

We have already looked at the example of Deborah. She is probably the best example because she was married. Why is this important? It is a crucial point because the idea of women in leadership should not become a **single-girls-only-club**. I must remind you of the fact that every member of the image of God, or Godhead, is capable of leadership. Why would God create us in His image and then change the mold?

Phoebe

As we look at some of the female leaders in the Bible, I want to show you how easy it is for people to misconstrue what the writers were saying. To do this I want to present our next text.

> *1 Timothy 3:8-10 Deacons likewise must be men of dignity, not double-tongued, or addicted to much wine or fond of sordid gain, but holding to the mystery of the faith with a clear conscience. These men must also first be tested; then let them serve as deacons if they are beyond reproach.*

A deacon is a position of leadership. This is why Paul gives instructions concerning the appointing of deacons. On the first reading of this passage, it would seem that only men can qualify for this position. Notice the other verses concerning this position.

> *1 Timothy 3:12-13 Deacons must be husbands of only one wife, and good managers of their children and their own households. For those who have served well as deacons obtain for themselves a high standing and great confidence in the faith that is in Christ Jesus.*

It could be argued here that only men are able to serve in this capacity; could it not? It looks rock solid. Nonetheless, if you will notice, I have left one verse out. Let's take a look at it.

__1 Timothy 3:11__ Women must likewise be dignified, not malicious gossips, but temperate, faithful in all things.

Why is this verse thrown in between the last two sections? Could it be that women are included in this position? Do we have any examples in the Bible of women being in this position?

__Romans 16:1 (RSV)__ I commend to you our sister Phoebe, a deaconess of the church at Cenchre-ae,

Junia

__Romans 16:7__ Greet Andronicus and Junias, my kinsmen and my fellow prisoners, who are outstanding among the apostles, who also were in Christ before me.

There is some controversy concerning this verse. First, is the name Junia male or female? It is definitely female. The male version is Junias. What I find interesting is that a number of versions change it to the male version rather than holding to the original Greek word. It becomes clear as to why when you see that they are also called apostles. A woman apostle! This brings us to the second bit of controversy concerning this verse. Some versions use the term *"are noted among the apostles."* The Greek word rendered "outstanding," however, means to be "marked." Being marked among the apostles is to be considered an apostle.

Anna

__Luke 2:36-38__ And there was a prophetess, Anna the daughter of Phanuel, of the tribe of Asher. She was advanced in years and had lived with her husband seven years after her marriage, and then as a widow to the age of eighty-four. She never left the *temple, serving night and day with fastings and prayers. At that very moment she came up and began giving thanks to God, and continued to speak of Him to all those who were looking for the redemption of Jerusalem.*

Those who say women are not to hold a place of leadership have a problem when a woman, who is in a place of leadership, is revealed in the Bible. Again, would God do something that He is against? Not only this, but also Anna presents an even greater problem than that to her detractors. If we look at the verses previous to this verse, we get an idea of the setting.

Luke 2:25 *And there was a man in Jerusalem whose name was Simeon; and this man was righteous and devout, looking for the consolation of Israel; and the Holy Spirit was upon him.*

This all took place when Jesus was just eight days old. On the eighth day, every Jewish male was required by the Law of Moses to be brought to the temple in Jerusalem for circumcision. On this day there would also be a sacrifice given. This is the setting of this chapter. Whether they met Simeon in the temple in Jerusalem or somewhere else in the city is unclear. What is clear, however, is that Simeon was a prophet and Anna was a prophetess. They are both in the same location. The import of this is that if a man who holds the office of prophet is ministering alongside a woman who is called a prophetess, then we can make only two conclusions.

- ✓ They are in disobedience to the requirements of God for women, or
- ✓ God is not opposed to women in leadership.

Summation

God is not opposed to women in leadership. Yes, He created a divine order in marriage whereby a woman is to submit to the leadership of her husband. If the husband is properly fulfilling his role, however, he will be supportive of his wife's calling whether or not that means he takes a background role.

If a woman wants to pursue a calling of God and does not want the resistance of a husband whose ego cannot take being in the background, she should remain single. She has every right to pursue God's calling and gifting upon her life. Although, if you are already a wife, the responsibility of your call has fallen upon your husband. If he forbids it, then you are free from that call and your husband will then have to answer to God for his reasons of forbidding you.

In my experience it is usually the ego of man that gets in the way of God's calling. Some men are so puffed up in their own minds that for them to have wives who are better speakers or better theologians than they are it is an insult to him. These men are immature and putting their own quests for prominence in front of God's will.

On the other hand, when husbands see their wives as a part of the image of God, as someone who holds an essential part of ministry as a reflection of that image and who holds a part of the ministry of the one flesh, then, and only then, can they move as a single unit, as one flesh. That is the will of God for woman and for man.

Are There Apostles And Prophets Today?

Chapter Five

There have been numerous articles generated for public consumption that make the claim that the offices of prophet and apostle are no longer in existence in the Body of Christ today. In this chapter I will submit evidence from the Word of God to prove that, indeed, they do exist and that the burden of proof lies upon those who would say they do not exist rather than on those who say they do.

For me, I am no longer so quick to accept doctrine simply on the basis of my respect for a particular teacher. I realize and accept that this applies to my teaching as well. It only takes one or two times of being misled to cure you from just taking someone's word without investigating the subject yourself.

I now approach every subject with the Word of God, an open heart, and prayer. Even positions that I have held for many years, I put to the scrutiny of the Word. That means that I also do not expect anyone else to just accept what I say without investigating the subject himself or herself. You must do the study yourselves and I am confident that, as promised in the Bible, the Holy Spirit will lead you and guide you into all truth. God bless you and speak to you as you read this chapter.

The reason that I say the burden of proof lies on those who say prophets and apostles do not exist today is that God has always been the One that plainly establishes all of the gifts and callings of the Church. Likewise, God would also plainly state the cessation of such gifts since He is the One that established them in the first place. We can agree that God is the Establisher of all callings and gifts can we not?

It is in Him that we move, breathe, and have our being; Jesus plainly called the twelve "apostles." He also plainly called John the Baptist a "prophet." So, if these offices existed when Jesus walked this earth and He established His acceptance of such, when and where did He state the cessation of these two ministerial offices? Before making the decision to say that God changed something He previously established, one must show beyond any doubt that God was indeed the One Who has changed it.

In broaching this subject, I think it important that all sides be given audience without being censored. Truth is a good thing; therefore, we should not be afraid to show all sides to an argument. Truth has a knack for surfacing to the top. What I attempt to do is to reveal the arguments against these two callings existing today and offer my rebuttal to them.

Apostles

Argument Against Apostolic Office #1 - *The Apostolic Test or Qualification*

> *"Since there are qualifications for being an apostle given in the book of Acts and since these qualifications (a witness of Jesus after the resurrection) can no longer be met, it is therefore impossible for apostles to exist today."*

Supporting Scripture

> *Luke 24:46, 48 and He said to them, "Thus it is written, that the Christ would suffer and rise again*

*from the dead the third day..." "You are witnesses
of these things."*

Acts 1:22 *"... beginning with the baptism of John
until the day that He was taken up from us—one of
these must become a witness with us of His
resurrection."*

Rebuttal

The assumption of this argument is that the qualifications
given for being an apostle in Acts 1:22 is extended to all called to
the office of apostle. If this qualification is extended to all who
would take the office of apostle, then only those who were eye
witnesses of the resurrected Lord could qualify to take that office.
The second assumption is if the first assumption is correct, then
Jesus is either incapable or unwilling to show Himself to anyone,
thus this would cause the office of apostle to cease to exist.

The argument we must answer then is the first assumption.
It should be noted that we need to take Acts 1:22 in context and we
must have a good understanding of what an apostle is in order to
lay this argument to rest. First, apostle is from the Greek *apostolos*
and means "sent one." If one is sent, then it is necessary for
someone to have sent them. An apostle is one sent to do something
or represent someone. This begs the question, *"Who sent the first
twelve apostles?"* Of course, the answer to that is Jesus. Now we
will take into consideration the context of Acts 1:22. This verse is
in response to the failure of Judas to take his office.

Acts 1:16-22 *"Brethren, the Scripture had to be
fulfilled, which the Holy Spirit foretold by the mouth
of David concerning Judas, who became a guide to
those who arrested Jesus. For he was counted
among us and received his share in this*

ministry." (Now this man acquired a field with the price of his wickedness, and falling headlong, he burst open in the middle and all his intestines gushed out. And it became known to all who were living in Jerusalem; so that in their own language that field was called Hakeldama, that is, Field of Blood.) "For it is written in the book of Psalms, 'Let his homestead be made desolate, And let no one dwell in it'; and, **'Let another man take his office.'** *Therefore it is necessary that of the men who have accompanied us all the time that the Lord Jesus went in and out among us— beginning with the baptism of John until the day that He was taken up from us—one of these must become a witness with us of His resurrection."*

Notice that I have highlighted the phrase *"Let another man take his office."* The eleven apostles understood the necessity of having twelve apostles to start the Church. Twelve is the number of government. Jacob had twelve sons who became the nation of Israel. Even Ishmael had twelve sons who would become twelve princes and a great nation. Jesus chose twelve and now there are only eleven.

In order to choose the person who would be able to take the office **Judas forfeited**, he must fit the qualification given in verse twenty-two. Since Jesus is the One who is sending the twelve, then there must be the qualification of being an eye witness of His resurrection. They had to have heard the command to *"go into all the world and make disciples of every nation."* Additionally, notice an even more important qualification in verse twenty-one. The person who was to take this important place was to have been with the eleven from the time of John the Baptist to the ascension.

This would make perfect sense since Jesus is the One who mentored them and was sending the twelve sent ones or apostles. Jesus would not sanction the sending of one who was not a disciple of His training and who did not receive the same equipping as the other eleven disciples. It would NOT make sense then that this qualification be extended beyond the twelve.

In fact, we will see later that the Apostle Paul would be disqualified from being an apostle if these qualifications were applied to him. There is another reason for this qualification to be instituted in order to replace Judas. The Apostle Paul called the twelve, *"most-eminent"* or *"super-apostles."*

> *2 Corinthians 11:5 For I consider myself not in the least inferior to the most **eminent apostles.***

> *2 Corinthians 12:11 I have become foolish; you yourselves compelled me. Actually I should have been commended by you, for in no respect was I inferior to the most **eminent apostles**, even though I am a nobody.*

Why are the twelve called super-apostles? Well, we have a few clues as to that reason. First, Jesus said that the twelve apostles would sit on twelve thrones and judge the twelve tribes of Israel. For this reason, they must be of the House of Israel.

> *Matthew 19:28 And Jesus said to them, "Truly I say to you, that you who have followed Me, in the regeneration when the Son of Man will sit on His glorious throne, you also shall sit upon twelve thrones, judging the twelve tribes of Israel.*

This shows us the importance and necessity of having twelve, not eleven, apostles. God chose at its inception that the nation of Israel would be composed of twelve tribes based upon the twelve sons of Jacob. God also chose that there would be twelve apostles who would be the starting point of His nation, the Church.

Second, when John was describing the New Jerusalem, which will come down from heaven at the end of the age, the wall of the city had twelve foundation stones upon which were written the names of the twelve apostles whereas the twelve gates were named after the twelve tribes of Israel.

> *Revelation 21:14 And the wall of the city had twelve foundation stones, and on them were the twelve names of the twelve apostles of the Lamb.*

These two honors, judging the twelve tribes of Israel and being written on the twelve stones of the new temple, are bestowed only on the original twelve apostles and are the very reasons that they are singled out as being the super-apostles. Now having established this fact, is it any wonder that the qualifications for becoming one of the TWELVE apostles were such that they had to have been with the other eleven and Jesus from the time of the baptism of Jesus by John the Baptist, which marked the start of His earthly ministry? Furthermore, they had to have been an eye witness of His resurrection which marked the end of His earthly ministry.

These clearly are not qualifications for all apostles, but rather they are just for the replacement of Judas. This replacement apostle would sit upon a throne to judge a tribe of Israel. This replacement apostle would have his name written on the foundation stone of the wall of the new city Jerusalem. This replacement apostle would be a sent one from Jesus' earthly ministry. Therefore, it is understandable that someone would have to be picked who would have sat under the teaching of Jesus for the same length of time as the other eleven had. In addition, since the whole of the Christian faith and doctrine were to issue out of these twelve men, it is then understandable why they had to have been eyewitnesses to the resurrection of Jesus.

> *Matthew 16:17-19 (KJV) And Jesus answered and said unto him, Blessed art thou, Simon Barjona: for flesh and blood hath not revealed it unto thee, but my Father which is in heaven. And I say also unto thee, That thou art Peter, and upon this rock I will build my Church; and the gates of hell shall not prevail against it. And I will give unto thee the keys of the kingdom of heaven: and whatsoever thou shalt bind on earth shall be bound in heaven: and whatsoever thou shalt loose on earth shall be loosed in heaven.*

What was the rock upon which Jesus declares that He will build His Church? It is the confession of Peter, who said of Jesus, *"Thou art the Christ, the Son of the living God."* In keeping with this theme, the foundation upon which Jesus builds His Church is the confession of who He is.

The argument against apostles existing today takes a disingenuous turn. Of course, the question will arise, *"What about the Apostle Paul?"* It is that question which causes them to only list the qualification of being an eye witness of the resurrection of Jesus so that they can quote the following verse.

> *1 Corinthians 9:1 Am I not free? Am I not an apostle? Have I not seen Jesus our Lord? Are you not my work in the Lord?*

They have the proof of this text, implying that Paul saw the Lord and, therefore, was qualified to be an apostle. Nevertheless, we must ask the question, *"Was Paul with the twelve super-*

apostles from the time Jesus was baptized?" The detractors to the apostolic ministry in the Church today only draw attention to being an eyewitness of the resurrection of Jesus as being a qualification to being an apostle. Why?

It is because this is the only way they can transfer that qualification on to all apostles; namely, Paul was undoubtedly called an apostle and he did see the Lord Jesus. However, Paul did not become a follower of Jesus until after His resurrection. Thus, Paul does not qualify to be an apostle according to the conditions stated in Acts, although the Bible clearly calls him an apostle. Therefore, if we were to apply the qualifications given by the eleven apostles in Acts 1:16-22 to the Apostle Paul, he would be disqualified! Nowhere do we see these qualifications used to qualify any of the other apostles, including Paul.

Moreover, none of the twelve apostles dispute that Paul was an apostle, which is significant since they were the ones who established the qualifications in the first place! Therefore, it is obvious that not all apostles who are named in the New Testament were with Jesus from the time of His baptism. It is this fact alone that proves that the qualifications mentioned in Acts chapter one are only for the replacement of Judas, who was a super-apostle, and are not qualifications for all apostles. Having destroyed the first assumption of argument one, the second assumption is irrelevant.

Also, note in I Corinthians 9:1 it is said that Paul was giving this evidence to support the fact that he was an apostle. The quote of I Corinthians 9:1 conveniently leaves out the very next verse that really is the statement that seals the apostleship of Paul. It wasn't seeing the Lord that sealed him as an apostle, but rather it was the existence of the Church of Corinth that sealed his apostleship. Let's read it.

1 Corinthians 9:2 If to others I am not an apostle, at least I am to you; for you are the seal of my apostleship in the Lord.

Paul's travel to Corinth, his teaching, and those who were converted to Christianity coalesced into a church and are what sealed his apostleship. If we use the qualification of seeing the resurrected Lord, then we also have to use the qualification of having been with Him from His baptism. The latter would disqualify Paul from being an apostle, but again, the Bible clearly calls him an apostle and to our knowledge the twelve super-apostles did not dispute this.

Argument 2 – Paul, the Last Apostle

"I Corinthians 15:8 states that Paul is the last apostle."

Supporting Scripture

1 Corinthians 15:8 and last of all, as to one untimely born, He appeared to me also.

Rebuttal

The quote of I Corinthians 15:8 lacks the burden of proof needed to establish the cessation of the office of apostle. Just because Paul said he was the last to see Jesus does not necessarily indicate that, number one, Jesus has not appeared to anyone since that time, or number two, that it was THE qualification upon which his apostleship rested.

Argument 3 – Paul Established the Bible

"Since 2 Peter 1:12 and 15 state that the truth had been firmly established and that all that is needed

from there forward is to remember them, therefore the office of apostle has ceased."

Supporting Scripture

2 Peter 1:12, 15 Therefore, I will always be ready to remind you of these things, even though you already know them, and have been established in the truth which is present with you... And I will also be diligent that at any time after my departure you will be able to call these things to mind.

Rebuttal

There are some truly big assumptions in this argument. The first assumption is that after the truth has been preached and established, there is no need for the office of an apostle. Nowhere can we read into that verse that Peter was saying he was the last apostle. It makes no sense, especially since others lived longer then he and there were others named as apostles after him.

If, after teaching someone some things from the Bible, I were to say to him that I would make sure he would be able to remember what I taught him after I were dead, what would you think I meant by that? To me, that simply means that the things I taught would be put in writing in order to be available after my death. It does not mean that there would be no more apostles. You just cannot read that into the verses.

It also seems to me that they are trying to say that modern day apostles and prophets are writing new doctrine. That is categorically incorrect! If anyone calls himself a prophet or apostle and tries to introduce new doctrine, then he is a false apostle or prophet. Remember, it was Apostle Paul who said that if anyone, even angels, delivered any other message then what he had delivered to the Church then let them be accursed.

Even the apostles were not delivering new doctrine. Everything they were teaching was already stated in the Old Testament scriptures, and Jesus taught them from the Old Testament before and after His resurrection. Even Jesus, who was God in the flesh, taught the truths that were written in the Old Testament. It is so much easier to let scripture say what it says without trying to read new meaning into it.

Argument 4 – Apostolic Foundation

> *"Ephesians 2:19-22 states that the Church is built upon the foundation of the apostles and prophets. Since we do not build foundations on the upper floors of a building, it is clear that apostles and prophets do not exist today."*

Supporting Scripture

> **Ephesians 2:19-22** *So then you are no longer strangers and aliens, but you are fellow citizens with the saints, and are of God's household, having been built on the foundation of the apostles and prophets, Christ Jesus Himself being the corner stone, in whom the whole building, being fitted together, is growing into a holy temple in the Lord, in whom you also are being built together into a dwelling of God in the Spirit.*

Rebuttal

The assumption of this argument is that **"foundation"** is equivalent to an *apostle and/or prophet*. Therefore, since the foundation has already been laid, there is no need for any other apostles or prophets. If we look at verse twenty-one, we see that we are talking about building a holy temple in the Lord. In verse twenty-two we find that it is people who are being built into a dwelling of God. Thus, the idea is that every building has a beginning and that beginning is the foundation. Notice that Jesus did not pick any prophets. He only picked apostles. How, then, can we speak of both apostles and prophets as being the foundation?

Prophets: The prophets were preaching the Good News before Jesus ever set foot on Earth, and thus, they equal one line of foundation stones.

Apostles: The apostles were preaching the Good News after Jesus left Earth and they represent the other line of foundation stones.

Jesus: The Cornerstone was the stone which intersects the two lines of foundation stones and from Whom they received the message of the Good News. A cornerstone was used to make sure that the rest of the stones were to be correct, level, and true.

Jesus was the Cornerstone Who connected the Old Testament prophets with the New Testament apostles. Thus, He is bringing together both Jews and Gentiles into one building, which is the context of verses 17 – 19. It was Jesus Who became the transition between the Old Testament and the New Testament, and between the Jews and the Gentiles. He had given the Old Testament prophets the revelations that they proclaimed as future events and to which the Jews arranged their lives. *("Jesus is the spirit of prophecy.")*

Jesus gave New Testament apostles as eyewitnesses to what those Old Testament prophets proclaimed and as those who brought the good news to the Gentiles. Jesus provided the truths and first principles upon which the Church was built. Those truths were proclaimed by the prophets, who did not even understand them. Then those truths were proclaimed and demonstrated by Jesus. Finally, those truths were proclaimed and demonstrated by the apostles, who were picked by Jesus to be eyewitnesses of these things and proclaim them to the world.

Therefore, the foundation represents the witness of the prophets and the resulting actions of the Jews before the time of Jesus, then the witness and demonstration of Jesus Himself, and finally the witness and demonstration of the apostles. The foundation does not represent just people, but truths upon which our faith relies.

Note that the prophets were empowered by the power of the Holy Spirit to prophecy. Jesus walked and spoke as God. The apostles were empowered by the Holy Spirit to witness. If the foundation represents the witness of the prophets, Jesus, and the apostles, then we are talking about truth and not the apostles and prophets themselves per say. In that, we have the same theme of a stone of witness that we found in the Old Testament.

> *Isaiah 28:15-16 (KJV) Because ye have said, We have made a covenant with death, and with hell are we at agreement; when the overflowing scourge shall pass through, it shall not come unto us: for we have made lies our refuge, and **under falsehood have we hid ourselves:** Therefore thus saith the Lord GOD, Behold, I lay in Zion for a foundation a **stone, a tried stone, a precious corner stone, a sure foundation: he that believeth shall not make haste.***

If the foundation represents teaching which produces action, then it has nothing to do with being apostles or prophets, but rather the teachings that they represented, presented, and demonstrated. This idea is further supported by looking at the context of the next chapter.

> **Ephesians 2:17-20** *And He came and **preached peace to you who were far away, and peace to those who were near;** for through Him **we both have our access** in one Spirit to the Father. So then you are no longer strangers and aliens, but you are fellow citizens with the saints, and are of God's household, having been built on the foundation of the apostles and prophets, Christ Jesus Himself being the corner stone...*

Jesus preached peace. The result was that both Jews and Gentiles became part of the household, or "temple," of God, having been built upon the foundation (teaching) of the apostles (for the Gentiles) and prophets (for the Jews) with Jesus being the chief cornerstone (Teacher) bringing them both together. Look at the following scripture:

> **2 Timothy 2:16-19** *But avoid worldly and empty chatter, for it will lead to further ungodliness, and their talk will spread like gangrene. Among them are Hymenaeus and Philetus, men who have gone astray from the truth saying that the resurrection has already taken place, and they upset the faith of some. **Nevertheless, the firm foundation of God stands**, having this seal, "The Lord knows those who are His," and, "Everyone who names the name of the Lord is to abstain from wickedness."*

When talking about falling away from the truth Paul says, nevertheless, the firm foundation of God stands. This again points to the idea of the foundation being truth, upon which Christians are to believe and act. In other words, it is *faith in the witness of God's Word.*

> **Luke 6:47-49** *"Everyone who comes to Me and* **hears My words and acts on them**, *I will show you whom he is like: he is like a man building a house, who dug deep and* **laid a foundation** *on the rock; and when a flood occurred, the torrent burst against that house and could not shake it, because it had been well built. But the one who has heard and has not acted accordingly, is like a man who built a house on the ground without any foundation; and the torrent burst against it and immediately it collapsed, and the ruin of that house was great."*

Note that following the Word is the difference between the house with the foundation and the house without the foundation. This shows us that the foundation described in Scripture is the idea of people hearing, believing, and then acting. That is the foundation of the apostles and the prophets.

> **1 Corinthians 3:11-15** *For no man can lay a* **foundation** *other than the one which is laid, which is Jesus Christ. Now if any man builds on the* **foundation** *with gold, silver, precious stones, wood, hay, straw, each man's work will become evident; for the day will show it because it is to be revealed with fire, and the fire itself will test the quality of each man's work. if any man's work which he has built on it remains, he will receive a reward. If any man's work is burned up, he will suffer loss; but he himself will be saved, yet so as through fire.*

Notice that the foundation is relevant to a person's work. How do we build upon the foundation? We do this by hearing, believing, and acting upon the Word of God. When you become a doer of the Word, you are actually building the holy temple of God. What would the wood, hay, and straw represent? These would represent actions taken either on a false concept or outside of faith.

All of that is said to prove that the prophets, Jesus, and apostles were responsible for laying the first principles of our faith. If the foundation is first principles, then it is not saying that apostles and prophets have ceased to exist. It must also be noted that in every verse I cited where the word "foundation" is used it is the same Greek word, *themelios*. This word is composed of the Greek word, *thema,* which is where we get the English word, "theme." A theme is an underlying or foundational topic found throughout a body of work. What is the underlying theme of the Old and New Covenants if it is not Jesus?

Summation

It should be clear to you that those who believe there are not apostles in the Church today have failed to provide ample evidence to support their theory. In fact, we have found that they purposely hide some Scriptures so that they can present an argument based upon partial information in order to achieve credibility in their arguments.

This practice only hurts their cause as they become deceivers rather than proclaiming the whole counsel of God. When we look at Ephesians chapter four we find ample evidence for the call and necessity of the apostles and prophets today.

> ***Ephesians 4:11-13*** *And He gave some as apostles, and some as prophets, and some as evangelists, and some as pastors and teachers, for the equipping of the saints for the work of service, to the building up*

of the body of Christ; until we all attain to the unity
of the faith, and of the knowledge of the Son of God,
to a mature man, to the measure of the stature
which belongs to the fullness of Christ.

If we ask some questions, I think we can get a clear picture of whether or not any of these callings have ceased. Jesus gave all five callings for some specific purposes. Let us see if these purposes have been fulfilled.

- Do the saints still need to be equipped or discipled?
- Does the Body of Christ still need to be built up?
- Do we still need to attain unity in the faith?
- Do we still need to attain the knowledge of the Son of God to the point of maturity?
- Do we still need to reach the measure of the fullness of Christ?

If we have answered those four questions in the affirmative, then we still need all five callings in the Church to function as God has ordained them to function.

Prophet

Argument 1 – Prophecy Has Ceased

"Since 1 Corinthians 13 states that "when that
which is perfect is come" prophecy will cease, then,
since "that which is perfect" is the Bible, which was
finished around 90 A. D., prophecy ceased at that
time. Also, since prophets prophesy and prophecy
has ceased, then prophets have ceased."

Supporting Scripture

> *1 Corinthians 13:8-10 Love never fails; but if there are gifts of prophecy, they will be done away; if there are tongues, they will cease; if there is knowledge, it will be done away. For we know in part and we prophesy in part; but when the perfect comes, the partial will be done away.*

Rebuttal

The great assumption of this argument is that the phrase *"that which is perfect"* is a reference to the canonized scripture, the Bible. Again, we must look at the context to gather what is being said.

> *1 Corinthians 13:8-12 Love never fails; but if there are gifts of prophecy, they will be done away; if there are tongues, they will cease; if there is knowledge, it will be done away. For we know in part and we prophesy in part; but when the perfect comes, the partial will be done away. When I was a child, I used to speak like a child, think like a child, reason like a child; when I became a man, I did away with childish things. For now we see in a mirror dimly, but **then** face to face; now I know in part, but **then** I will know fully just as I also have been fully known.*

We have only added two verses to achieve context. Verse twelve is the key to understanding this section. The phrase, *"then face to face,"* is pointing to a period in time that was previously discussed. It doesn't take much reading to realize that the word "then" is in reference to the time *"when the perfect comes."* If the "perfect" were the Bible, how would we come face to face with it? Does the Bible have a face?

The next "then" still points back to the time of *"when the perfect comes"* and suggests that at that time I will know fully just as I am fully known. Again, it does not make sense that we fully know the Bible just as we do not fully know Jesus. Although we have the Bible, but I don't know anyone who fully knows the Bible. We also have Jesus, but I do not know anyone who would claim to fully know Jesus.

> *1 John 3:2 Beloved, now we are children of God, and it has not appeared as yet what we will be. We know that when He appears, we will be like Him, because we will see Him just as He is.*

We will not fully know what we will be until we see Him, Jesus, Who is perfect. There are those who will say that the word "that" in the phrase *"that which is perfect"* is neuter in the Greek and therefore cannot refer to our Lord; otherwise, the word used should have been in the masculine gender. To that, we can appeal to another section of Scripture.

> *1 John 1:1 KJV That which was from the beginning, which we have heard, which we have seen with our eyes, which we have looked upon, and our hands have handled, of the Word of life;*

Here the word "that" is also in the neuter and clearly is referring to Jesus. It is somewhat disheartening that we have to get into the gender of Greek words to prove a doctrine. If a doctrine were so obscure that you need to appeal to the gender of Greek words, it would be best abandoned. When you see people needing to do gymnastics with the Word of God to make things fit, watch out!

I have found in my studies that all of the doctrines that are presented in the Word are done so in abundance. When you see the same principle over and over again in the Word, you have a doctrine that you can rely on as accurate. Another problem with this argument is that if we can show there are prophets after the 90 A. D. deadline given by those who seem to think this is when the prophetic office ceased, then their argument fails again. More importantly, if we can show Scripture declaring the prophetic office beyond this point, we have defeated this argument to the utmost.

> *Revelation 11:10 KJV And they that dwell upon the earth shall rejoice over them, and make merry, and shall send gifts one to another; because these two prophets tormented them that dwelt on the earth.*

Here we have a clear reference to two prophets in the time of the tribulation, which has not happened up to this point in time. If, therefore, God has done away with the prophetic office because we have the completed Bible, why are there prophets yet to come? They still have the Bible. In addition, we also have numerous mention of the prophetic office during the first Church age.

> *Acts 21:10-11 And as we were staying there for some days, a certain prophet named Agabus came down from Judea. And coming to us, he took Paul's belt and bound his own feet and hands, and said, "This is what the Holy Spirit says: 'In this way the Jews at Jerusalem will bind the man who owns this belt and deliver him into the hands of the Gentiles.'"*

> *Acts 11:28-30 And one of them named Agabus stood up and began to indicate by the Spirit that there would certainly be a great famine all over the*

world. And this took place in the reign of Claudius.
And in the proportion that any of the disciples had
means, each of them determined to send a
contribution for the relief of the brethren living in
Judea. And this they did, sending it in charge of
Barnabas and Saul to the elders.

Acts 2:17-18 KJV And it shall come to pass in the
last days, saith God, I will pour out of my Spirit
upon all flesh: and your sons and your daughters
shall prophesy, and your young men shall see
visions, and your old men shall dream dreams: 18
And on my servants and on my handmaidens I will
pour out in those days of my Spirit; and they shall
prophesy:

Are we not in the last days? We should not see a cessation
of prophecy as the end approaches, but rather an increase in
prophecy. It should become more established in the Church as the
day approaches. I choose to believe the Word of God.

Argument 2 – Prophets Are Preachers

"Since the word "prophecy" means to speak forth,
anyone who preaches the Word of God is speaking
forth and thus they are prophets. Prophets do not
predict the future any longer."

Rebuttal

The assumption of this argument is that the definition of
the word, "prophecy," is "to speak forth" and could not mean
"to predict the future." This is a very weak argument and it has
been passed around so often that many have believed it without
investigating its merits. There are some devious practices taking

place in this argument and I want to bring light to them. First, let us look at the definition of the Greek word for prophecy.

4395 *[propheteuo /prof·ate·**yoo**·o/] v. **1** to prophesy, to be a prophet, speak forth by divine inspirations, to predict. **1a** to prophesy. **1b** with the idea of foretelling future events pertaining esp. to the kingdom of God.*

4396 *[prophetes /prof·**ay**·tace/] n m. **1** in Greek writings, an interpreter of oracles or of other hidden things. **2** one who, moved by the Spirit of God and hence his organ or spokesman, solemnly declares to men what he has received by inspiration, especially concerning future events, and in particular such as relate to the cause and kingdom of God and to human salvation.*

4253 *[pro /pro/] prep. A primary preposition **1** before.*

5346 *[phemi /fay·**mee**/] v. **1** to make known one's thoughts, to declare. **2** to say.* [15]

The Greek word for prophet and prophecy is made up of two Greek words. I put those definitions in (4253 and 5346) so that you can see its true meaning. As you can see, the Greek shows us that the compound word that makes up the word "prophecy" is to "say before." It is clear from this definition that, indeed, prophecy has the meaning of declaring an event before it happens. If we look

---

[15] *(Strong, J., 1996)*

at how this word is used in the New Testament, it becomes completely clear that this is the case.

> *Matthew 13:14-15* *"In their case the prophecy of Isaiah is being fulfilled, which says, 'You will keep on hearing, but will not understand; You will keep on seeing, but will not perceive; For the heart of this people has become dull, With their ears they scarcely hear, And they have closed their eyes, Otherwise they would see with their eyes, Hear with their ears, And understand with their heart and return, And I would heal them.'*

If what Isaiah said would happen in the future has already happened and they call it prophecy, it is clear that prophecy is declaring future events. The Church still needs the prophetic. Agabus warned of a famine so that the Church was able to start saving for the event and the church members would not suffer. Are we not still in need of these community kinds of warnings? Agabus warned Paul what was to happen to him when he went to Jerusalem. Do we not still need these personal warnings?

Then how do they get the definition "to speak forth?" Here is where the deception takes place. As I have shown, the Greek prefix "pro" means "before." However, the Latin prefix "pro" means "forth." Therefore, in order to get this word to mean "to speak forth," they substitute the Greek prefix with the Latin prefix.

DEFINITION

pro-1 *pref. **1.** Acting in the place of; substituting for: pronoun. **2.** Supporting; favoring: prorevolutionary. [Middle English, from Old French, from Latin pro-, pro-, from pro, for.*

pro-2pref. ***1.*** *Earlier; before; prior to:*
procambium. Rudimentary: pronucleus. ***2.***
Anterior; in front of: procephalic.[Middle
English, from Old French, from Greek, from pro,
before, in front. See ***per1****.]*[16]

Argument 3 – The Warning of False Prophets

"Since the Word has so many warnings against
false prophets and false apostles, this shows us that
they, the real ones, do not exist in the modern
Church."

Rebuttal

The Bible does say to beware of **false** prophets and **false**
apostles, which in and of itself is a statement to the validity of
modern day prophets and apostles. If there are false prophets, one
must conclude that there are genuine ones, too. Using their logic, I
could conclude that since the Word says in Galatians 1:8 that we
are to reject anyone preaching any other gospel means that all
modern day preachers are false simply because they are preaching.
This simply does not make sense.

Notice in the book of Revelation in Jesus' message to the
churches that He tells one group that they have tested those who
call themselves apostles when they are not. He commends them for
this practice. If the office of apostle and prophet have ceased, why
would we need to test them? We would know that they were false
based upon the proclamation of their call if that call no longer

---

[16] *(American Heritage Dictionary, 1997)*

existed. Therefore, if the call did not exist there would be no reason to test them.

One of the conclusions they mistakenly make is that modern day apostles and prophets are adding to or taking away from the Word, which was already established by the first apostles and prophets. That is simply not true. Apostle and prophet callings are not to establish new doctrine or new scripture. True modern day apostles and prophets would reject any attempt to do so.

> *1 Corinthians 14:3 But one who prophesies speaks to men for edification and exhortation and consolation.*

> *1 Corinthians 14:31-33 For you can all prophesy one by one, so that all may learn and all may be exhorted; and the spirits of prophets are subject to prophets; for God is not a God of confusion but of peace, as in all the Churches of the saints.*

> *1 Timothy 4:14 Do not neglect the spiritual gift within you, which was bestowed upon you through prophetic utterance with the laying on of hands by the presbytery.*

Here we see the purposes and the reasons we still need prophecy today. You must ask the question, *"Do we still need these things today?"* In addition, we get the idea by the way those verses read that prophecy is something that is continuous. There are no instances of Jesus saying that these callings and gifts will cease before He returns. Let us then embrace them and cultivate them so that our lives will be fuller and enhanced by the Lover of our souls, Jesus the Christ!

Summation

There can be no other conclusion, other than we are to accept the five gifts that Jesus gave to the Church; to equip the saints for works of service to bring unity and maturity to the Body of Christ. If we deny any one of them, we shortchange the Church. Let us go forward and proclaim unashamedly the fullness of the five fold ministries. We start by looking at the ministry of the apostle and what this calling brings to the Body of Christ.

The Apostle

T he ministries of the apostle and the prophet have been neglected in the Church for hundreds of years. It is our hope that in studying these two ministries we will again bring attention to them so that they could once again take their position in the Church as God has so ordained they should. Even though there has been a move to suppress these two callings, they have nevertheless continued to operate even if under different names and positions. You can refuse who a person is, but you cannot change who God created them to be. You can say their gift does not exist, but that does not negate or cancel it.

In studying the five ministries, it must be restated that Christ is always the Head of His Church and that it is He Who gave the five ministries as gifts to the Church. He did not set up those in the Church in a hierarchical order of authority, but placed them shoulder to shoulder to equip the saints to do the work of God. We do see a sequence of callings, but this is to facilitate the proper functioning and stability of the Church and is not intended as a chain of command.

The Five Ministries

> *Ephesians 4:11 And He gave some as **apostles**, and some as prophets, and some as evangelists, and some as pastors and teachers...*

It is important to note that the five ministries are tasked by God to equip. This means that the disciple, or student, is getting something from the minister, but it is not enough just to get something. Inherent in the equipping process is the duty of the one being equipped to accept and begin to put into practice what they are receiving. A soldier can be given body armor and a firearm, but if he does not put on the armor and pick up the firearm he remains unequipped. A soldier can also receive specialized training for combat, but if during combat he does not employ that training, then it has not benefited him at all. Likewise, the disciple who refuses to implement what he or she has learned cannot be equipped against his or her will.

For instance, a prophet can equip you with the knowledge of your call, but it is up to you to start the process of undertaking that call. If you don't walk in the direction revealed by the prophet, you will not realize the call. A teacher can equip you with an important biblical concept, but if you don't hear it and do it, you will not realize the benefit of that equipping. Each five fold ministry calling has a portion in the equipping process of the disciple. Nonetheless, incumbent upon the disciple is the energetic persistent action to put into performance what they have received.

There are some things in the equipping process, like anointings or gifts, that are transferable without the disciple's action. When the Spirit of God places upon the heart of the leadership to lay hands upon a disciple, there is in that moment transference of anointing, gifting, or both to accomplish the task for which the disciple is being sent out for.

> *1 Timothy 4:14 Do not neglect the spiritual gift within you, which was bestowed on you **through prophetic utterance with the laying on of hands by the presbytery**.*

We must caution, however, that not all anointing and gifting come in this way of laying on of hands. These are special moments dictated by the Divine Spirit to impart something into the disciple. For the most part, the equipping process is learning-oriented. That is, the maturing process of the disciple is accomplished through the hearing of and believing in the Word of God. Jesus prepared and matured His disciples through the learning process.

> *John 8:31-32 So Jesus was saying to those Jews who had believed Him, "**If you continue in My word**, then you are truly disciples of Mine; and you will know the truth, and the truth will make you free."*

There were times when Jesus laid hands upon His disciples to impart something, but it was confined to the sending out of that disciple to do a work. What we see, though, as a dominant paradigm in the charismatic church of today, is the idea that one can receive everything he needs for ministry through the laying on of hands and prophecy. Never does the Scripture give us this indication. There is throughout Scripture a **premium** put on increasing in the knowledge of God through His word in order to mature the saint.

> *2 Timothy 3:16-17 All Scripture is inspired by God and profitable for teaching, for reproof, for correction, for training in righteousness; so that the man of God may be adequate, **equipped** for every good work.*

Lest there be any confusion to the equipping process, let me reiterate that without biblical training in the Scriptures, there is no equipping taking place. Each calling (apostle, prophet, evangelist, pastor, or teacher) will use the Scriptures to equip the saints in order to set them on the good path of their call that they may accomplish the good work for which they are destined.

*Hebrews 13:20-21 Now the God of peace, who brought up from the dead the great Shepherd of the sheep through the blood of the eternal covenant, even Jesus our Lord, **equip** you in every good thing to do His will, working in us that which is pleasing in His sight, through Jesus Christ, to whom be the glory forever and ever. Amen.*

What is an "*Apostle?*"

Before we can tackle the five ministry gifts to the Church, we must understand that Jesus was all five ministries in bodily form, authority, and anointing. When Jesus ascended to the Father, He divided that mantle of authority into five separate equipping ministries (apostle, prophet, teacher, evangelist, and pastor). When all five ministries are functioning in the Church, the Church is able to increase with authority and power because the image of Christ is being represented and presented to the saints in complete form. Note that Jesus called all twelve disciples "apostles." This becomes clear when we understand the ministry of the apostle as understood by the Hebrew culture.

"QUOTE"

Apostle (Greek ..."to send"), a person delegated for a certain purpose; ...one invested with representative power. "Apostoloi" was the official name given to the men sent by the rulers of Jerusalem to collect the half-shekel tax for the Temple, the tax itself being called "apostolé." The emperor Honorius, in his edict of 399, mentions "...the elders and those whom the Jews call apostoloi, who are sent forth by the patriarch at a certain season of the year to collect silver and gold from the various synagogues." [17]

All twelve disciples were to be "sent ones." What were they sent to do? According to Jesus, they were sent to make disciples. This was the inception of the Church. There cannot be a church without an apostle who was sent to build it. As Paul said to the Corinthians, *"you are my seal of apostleship"* (1 Corinthians 9:2).

Consequently, it was a continuation of the divine plan of God. God "sent" His Son, "The Apostle," Who equipped the twelve disciples as apostles and "sent" them to make disciples who would then be "sent" to repeat the procedure. Jesus did not come to build His Church directly, but indirectly through His servants. Therefore, His twelve disciples were all apostles and all had the duty and call to build the Church. From the original twelve disciples came the equipping of all other apostles as well as prophets, teachers, pastors, and evangelists.

The historicity of the apostle is in line with what Jesus had in mind in His naming the twelve as apostles. Specifically, the apostle was tasked as a teacher who was responsible to collect the *apostole*, or temple tax. The temple tax was a tariff levied by the Sanhedrin to build and maintain the temple and the synagogues. Note that in the book of Acts people were bringing their gifts and placing them at the apostles' feet. Note also that Paul was tasked with getting gifts from a church in one region to relieve a church in another area. In addition, all of the accounts of apostles being sent out reveal that they were sent out in pairs of two.

---

[17] –*Jewish Encyclopedia* (Jewish Encyclopedia, 1901-1906)

*"At the feet of the apostles" were laid the
contributions of the early Christians to their
common treasury, exactly as was done in the year
of release in every city and in every Essene
community. **"Two and two"** the apostles were
enjoined to travel (Mark 6:7; Luke 10:2), exactly
as was the rule among the charity-workers...
Thus Paul always traveled in the company of
either Barnabas or Silas (Acts 11:30; 12:25;
15:25, 30), and was entrusted with the charitable
gifts collected for the brethren in Jerusalem (see
also I Cor. 16:1; II Cor. 8:4, 9:5; Rom. 15:25;
Gal. 2:10); while Barnabas traveled also with
Mark (Acts 15:39, 40).* [18]

What does an Apostle do?

*1 Corinthians 12:28 And God has appointed in the
Church, first apostles, second prophets, third
teachers, then miracles, then gifts of healings,
helps, administrations, various kinds of tongues.*

Since prophets, teachers, pastors, and evangelists are not
"builders" in the Church, all of Jesus' disciples were apostles. It is
not that the other ministries do not assist in the building of the
Church, but the apostle has the gifting, anointing, and the task to
begin this process and see it through to completion; whereas, the
other ministries assist in building the Church through the gifting
and anointing needed to maintain and grow it. It is for this reason
that apostles are mentioned first in succession. It is not to suggest

---

[18] *(Jewish Encyclopedia, 1901-1906)*

authority over the others, but the necessity of this ministry to be first in constructing the building by acquiring finances and laying the groundwork.

You should not start the construction of a building without the correct contractors to do the work. To start the building process well, one should follow the correct order of proper construction practices. It is first necessary to acquire and survey the land, then different builders are contracted before actually beginning the building process.

There are even times when demolition is needed prior to construction. That is, there are other structures in that region that need to be demolished before a new structure can be built. Once this demolition takes place the excavators can come in and prepare the land for building. Without the surveyors and excavators, there can be no need for the plumber, carpenter, or electrician since there would be no building.

This is evidenced in Acts 17:23, which describes how Paul was traveling through Athens, Greece. At that time the Athenians had an idol, or god, for every occasion. To come there and preach the true God would only be seen as another god. Paul then has to strategically approach them in order to deconstruct, or demolish the Athenians' idea of God. To do this, he appeals to one of their idols called, *"THE UNKNOWN GOD."* Paul then says I have come to reveal Him to you. Some of Paul's listeners began to sneer at him, but others believed and began to follow the true God of Whom Paul spoke. Thus, the Church was born in that area.

Notice, though, that Paul first surveyed the land to see what that culture believed. Armed with that information he was able to develop a strategy and parlay it into an appeal to believe in the true God. Paul even quoted from that culture's renowned poets. Here we see the action of a true apostle of God and the fruit of his labor was a handful of believers.

There are certain teachings concerning the apostle that need to be addressed. Many associate them with a *first-in–command* position in the Church and they use 1 Corinthians 12:28 to support this position. If this verse were talking about a succession of authority, why would it mention gifts in the listing? What authority do gifts possess? Secondly, where are the evangelists and pastors? Are they relegated to be under the authority of miracles?

It makes much more sense to see this verse as a building process. We really see a pattern of apostle and prophet teams in building a new church. First, there must be the apostle; the apostle is sent to survey the land, raise funds to build, and contract believers to function in their call to work. Once the land is surveyed the prophet will first demolish any old structures that may be in the way to make room for the excavation process to begin, as well as develop the vision that the new structure will take. Next, the teacher is needed to give instruction for the erection of the building. Therefore, the succession, or order of the callings in this verse is not to show authority, but the necessity of order for the building process.

Anytime we see a hierarchical order established there are **always** those who want to grab for position and power. Although, when ministers recognize the differences of the callings in one another, true leadership can emerge as each leader defers to the gifting in the other leaders. Can you imagine the plumber being jealous of the electrician and trying to wire the building?

How Would I Recognize This Call in Myself or Others?

> **Galatians 1:1** *Paul, an apostle (not sent from men nor through the agency of man, but through Jesus*

Christ and God the Father, who raised Him from the dead),

First, it must be noted that apostles are neither self-made nor self-proclaimed. There are those who confer upon themselves the title of apostle, thinking that they are elevating themselves to the top in the chain of command. These are to be avoided since they are not sent ones for they do not submit to the Head Who is Christ and they were not sent out by the Church through the direction of the Holy Spirit. Even Apostle Paul was trained and equipped into the Christian faith by the appearance of Jesus and the Antioch church.

> *Galatians 1:15-18 But when God, who had set me apart even from my mother's womb and called me through His grace, was pleased to reveal His Son in me so that I might preach Him among the Gentiles, I did not immediately consult with flesh and blood, nor did I go up to Jerusalem to those who were apostles before me; but I went away to Arabia, and returned once more to Damascus. Then three years later I went up to Jerusalem to become acquainted with Cephas, and stayed with him fifteen days.*

> *Galatians 1:11-12 For I would have you know, brethren, that the gospel which was preached by me is not according to man. For I neither received it from man, nor was I taught it, but I received it through a revelation of Jesus Christ.*

Paul submitted to the church leadership at Antioch and then, when the time was right, the Holy Spirit sent him out.

> *Acts 13:1-5 Now there were at Antioch, in the Church that was there, **prophets and teachers**:*

Barnabas, and Simeon who was called Niger, and
Lucius of Cyrene, and Manaen who had been
*brought up with Herod the tetrarch, and **Saul**.*
While they were ministering to the Lord and fasting,
the Holy Spirit said, "Set apart for Me Barnabas
and Saul for the work to which I have called them."
Then, when they had fasted and prayed and laid
their hands on them, they sent them away. So, being
sent out by the Holy Spirit, they went down to
Seleucia and from there they sailed to Cyprus.
When they reached Salamis, they began to proclaim
the word of God in the synagogues of the Jews; and
they also had John as their helper.

What is interesting in this passage of Scripture is that it begins by listing the prophets and teachers who were in the Antioch church. Note the conspicuous absence of the application of the term apostle. Paul, or Saul, was a teacher and we find this in another passage.

> ***2 Timothy 1:10-11*** *but now has been revealed by*
> *the appearing of our Savior Christ Jesus, who*
> *abolished death and brought life and immortality to*
> *light through the gospel, for which I was appointed*
> *a **preacher and an apostle and a teacher**.*

We do not find the term apostle being associated with Paul until:

> ***Acts 14:14*** *But when the **apostles** Barnabas and*
> *Paul heard of it, they tore their robes and rushed*
> *out into the crowd, crying out...*

Paul was a teacher in the church at Antioch, but when the Holy Spirit set him and Barnabas apart to be **sent out**, then as a "sent one" with the blessings and prayers of his home church, he became an apostle to the region to which he was sent.

Passion

An apostle's intense desire is to **establish churches**. Those churches then become like children to that apostle. When the apostle leaves and goes on to establish another church, he continues to monitor what he has already established. As we see with Paul, he would send people out to each one of the churches that he had established to observe and report back to him on how those churches were doing. Once Paul had that report, he would send off a letter to commend and admonish them according to their condition.

There is a deep passion in the heart of the apostle for **correct doctrine** and the health of the Church. One cannot build a church unless it is built upon the confession that Jesus is the Christ, the Son of the living God. Anything that seeks to tear away at this confession will cause the apostle of that church to rise up in anger against the one presenting it. Paul describes it as wolves entering in among them. This is an apt picture of the passion Paul had for the Church.

> *Galatians 5:12 I wish that those who are troubling you would even mutilate themselves.*

> *Galatians 3:1 You foolish Galatians, who has bewitched you, before whose eyes Jesus Christ was publicly portrayed as crucified?*

> *Acts 20:29-30 I know that after my departure savage wolves will come in among you, not sparing the flock; and from among your own selves men will arise, speaking perverse things, to draw away the disciples after them.*

The apostle has a **father's heart** for his own disciples and for the churches that he has established. The apostle, like a father, also has a deep desire to reveal God the Father's heart to them. Being a father means that you are concerned with every aspect of the life for which you are a father. That means you will be fiercely protective over your children and will be ready to demolish anything that seeks to destroy them.

The dilemma with regard to understanding the different callings is that each calling requires different very deep passions that are necessary for excellence. If we judge these passions from the aspect of our own call, which may be different, we can become critical of the other callings. This is why it is necessary to understand the zealous passions of all five callings so that we are not offended or confused by them, but rather we celebrate and encourage that passion in each person, knowing that it is for the health and benefit of the body.

What Kind of Gifts do Apostles Exhibit?

The apostle will have gifts that help him fulfill his calling. Since the apostle sets up churches, he will have the gift of **administration**. He will be able to establish a core group and structure them in a way that gives them form and purpose. Moreover, since he will be putting others in positions in that body to nurture and train the body, he will have the ability to recognize callings in others and bring them to a place where they can fulfill that calling.

It is important to note that there is a vast difference in moving in a spiritual gift and the gifting that comes with the call to an office of ministry. Whereas the Holy Spirit will move for the moment in anyone in the Body through a spiritual gift, the one called to the office of ministry operates in that gift at all times. In their private time they are operating in that gifting, as well as in the time at work in the ministry. **This gifting can be misinterpreted as a talent for something else.**

The apostle has the gift of administration. If that person does not understand what his call is, he will use that gift in other endeavors. I have often seen and read of those called to be an apostle feeling like they are suddenly called to the political arena or they are suddenly called to go into business. This is not to say that God does not call them to do different things; it is just a temptation because of the perceived natural abilities of God's gifting that person has.

The apostle has the gift of **teaching**. Since the apostle is so concerned with doctrine, teaching is a gift that allows him to make sense of the good news to others. Going into regions where the people may have never heard the good news requires one to be able to communicate to the people in the context of the cultural peculiarities in that region. That is why the apostle is strategic and surveys the land before going forward. He must be able to communicate in a language that would be understood by the inhabitants of that land.

What Does it Mean to be an "Apostolic Church?"

The term "apostolic church" is related to the idea of the meaning of the word "apostle" and not that it is a church with apostles in it. The concept is that the true, New Testament Church was one in which they equipped and then sent out (apostolic) teams that would take the gospel to other areas. All churches should be "sending-out churches" at some point in their development.

On the other hand, the model we see in churches today is the opposite of that. Now it seems the objective is to get active members into the Church and then to keep them seated there for the rest of their lives. An apostolic church desires to send people out, not only in the field of ministry to build new works, but also to send them out into the marketplace to take the kingdom of God into the varying components of society. These people should still come back to their home church, but they should be active in the work for which God called them.

If we are ever to become the Church that Jesus fashioned us to be, we must be a Church that is "outward" oriented to minister to the local community and unto the uttermost parts of the world. The apostolic ministry is best suited to fulfill that endeavor.

In Conclusion

Since apostles are the first in building a church, so to speak, what a tragedy that many organizations do not accept this call. To establish churches in other regions, they send out what they call "missionaries" or "church planters." It may be that these missionaries and church planters have an apostolic call, but they are hardly recognized as such.

The Prophet

Chapter Seven

The prophet is one of the most interesting studies among the five callings. There is an abundance of prophets from which to study in the Old Testament, whereas, the New Testament has an abundance of apostles. Prophets wrote most of the books of the Old Testament, but apostles wrote most of the books of the New Testament.

Prophets can be found in the New Testament, but there is not much written about them. What we do find in the New Testament is an abundance of information about the primary gift of the prophet, which is prophecy. We have plenty of information to draw the necessary conclusions concerning this interesting call.

The prophetic ministry is tasked with revealing the heart and purposes of God to both individuals and to organizations whether it is a church, a city, or a nation. If we do not accept this extremely important ministry we will lack a very important component in understanding and following the will of God.

What is a Prophet?

> *Ephesians 4:11 And He gave some as apostles, and some as **prophets**, and some as evangelists, and some as pastors and teachers...*

The prophet is an important component in the function and direction of a church. Many have tried to redefine them to fit a culture which has rejected the ministry of the prophet. Often times Christians are embarrassed even at the mention of someone being a prophet today. On the other hand, there is not that same stigmatism associated with fortunetellers or psychics.

The enemy works against the prophet diligently, I think, because they are often the ones who first notice his workings. Thus, the enemy has succeeded in nullifying this ministry by bringing reproach upon it. Likewise, there are also many false prophets who have brought blight upon the calling of the prophet. What we must do in an honest look at prophets today is to remember that we cannot judge the whole of something by sampling only a small portion. What I hope to do in this lesson is to not only teach what the prophet is, but also to bring a sense of understanding back to the prophetic office. Hopefully, this will encourage you to accept this ministry as a needed and valid ministry in the Church today.

QUOTE

> With the idea of a prophet there was this necessarily attached, that he spoke not his own words, but those which he had divinely received, and that he was the messenger of God, and the declarer of his will; this is clear from a passage of peculiar authority in this matter. [19]

I will only be giving the definition of *"prophecy"* rather than *"prophet"* because a prophet is defined by what he does, and that is he gives prophecy. If you only look up the Hebrew word for prophet you will only get the term prophet. This is just like the apostle who is a sent one. To be sent out is the action of the apostle; to prophesy is the action of the prophet. The root word of

---

[19] Gesenius, 2003

Hebrew for prophet is prophecy, whereas in the Greek the root word for prophecy is prophet.

HEBREW Definition: Prophecy

> *TO CAUSE TO BUBBLE UP, hence to pour forth words abundantly, as is done by those who speak with ardour or divine emotion of mind.*[20]

From this definition I get the picture of a glass of milk with a straw in it and someone blowing through the straw causing the milk to produce bubbles. The breath, or Spirit of God, is moving in humans to cause them to say what He is saying.

> *2 Peter 1:20-21 But know this first of all, that no prophecy of Scripture is a matter of one's own interpretation, for no prophecy was ever made by an act of human will, **but men moved by the Holy Spirit spoke from God.***

Someone may ask, *"How does that differ from a pastor preaching a sermon? Didn't he get his sermon from God?"* The answer is that the difference is a pastor will often get a subject or title and then God anoints them to preach a sermon about it. In doing this the pastor will add his own speech and words, then throw in an illustration, and we have a sermon. The prophet is different, though, in that every word spoken in the name of God is to be from the mouth of God.

There has been a move in Christendom to relegate the prophet to just being a preacher. This does not stand up to the Hebrew understanding of the word and it especially does not stand

---

[20] Gesenius, 2003

up to the Greek understanding of the word. Another word in the Old Testament for prophet is *"seer."* It simply means *"vision."* To put this in perspective read the following:

> **1 Samuel 9:9** *(Formerly in Israel, when a man went to inquire of God, he used to say, "Come, and let us go to the seer"; for he who is called a prophet now was formerly called a seer.)*

Now compare that with:

> **Numbers 12:6** *He said, "Hear now My words: If there is a prophet among you, I, the Lord, shall make Myself known to him in a vision. I shall speak with him in a dream.*

So the term "seer" is used to describe those who see visions and dreams. What is important to note is that "prophet" and "seer" are synonymous.

GREEK DEFINITION: PROPHET

prophḗtēs *[prophet]*, **prophḗtis** *[prophetess]*, **prophēteúō** *[to prophesy]*, **prophēteía** *[prophecy]*, **prophētikós** *[prophetic]*, **pseudoprophḗtēs** *[false prophet]*

A. Secular Greek.

I. Linguistic Aspects.

1. The prefix pro- causes some ambiguity regarding the precise sense of prophḗtēs, but it would seem that the original sense in Greek is "one who proclaims," although soon the idea of "one who predicts" also occurs.

2. The word prophḗtis (from the end of the fifth century B.C.) is the feminine form.

3. The verb prophēteúō has the twofold sense "to proclaim" and "to be an oracle prophet."

4. prophēteía denotes a. "ability to declare the divine will," b. "proclamation," and c. "prophetic office."

5. prophētikós means "belonging to a prophet," "prophetic."

6. In the word pseudoprophḗtēs the first part can be an object ("prophet of lies") or it may be adjectival ("false prophet").[21]

This Greek word is a compound word made up of two words.

GREEK DEFINITION: PRO

4253 [pro /pro/] prep. A primary preposition; TDNT 6:683; TDNTA 935; GK 4574; 48 occurrences; AV translates as "before" 44 times, "above" twice, "above ... ago" once, and "or ever" once. 1 before.[22]

GREEK DEFINITION: PHEMI

5346 [phemi /fay·mee/] v. Properly, the same as the base of 5457 and 5316; GK 5774; 58 occurrences; AV translates as "say" 57 times,

---

[21] *(Kittel, 1995, c1985)*

[22] *(Strong, J., 1996)*

*and "affirm" once. 1 to make known one's
thoughts, to declare. 2 to say.* [23]

The idea of *prophetes* is "to declare before." This provides
us the indication of telling of future events. To **speak for** someone
does not necessarily denote speaking word for word and does not
necessarily carry with it the idea of the telling of future things.
Although, to **speak before** does carry the idea of the telling of
future things, and not only that, but also if we look at the context of
how the word is used, we can solidify its meaning.

What Does a Prophet Do?

It should be obvious from the previous section that
prophets prophesy, but there is much more. We must also deal with
the question: *"Are New Testament prophets like the Old Testament
prophets?"* I see no indication to suggest there is a difference
between the two. There is a movement in a number of prophetic
ministries to suppress the prophets to only prophesy good things.
This flies in the face of Scripture. The Scripture they use is the
following:

> *1 Corinthians 14:3 But one who prophesies speaks
> to men for edification and exhortation and
> consolation.*

Before we delve into this verse, I want to share with you
other Scriptures.

> *Isaiah 30:9-12 For this is a rebellious people, false
> sons, Sons who refuse to listen To the instruction of
> the Lord; Who say to the seers, "You must not see
> visions"; And to the prophets, "You must not*

---

[23] *(Kittel, 1995, c1985)*

prophesy to us what is right, Speak to us pleasant words, Prophesy illusions. Get out of the way, turn aside from the path, Let us hear no more about the Holy One of Israel." Therefore thus says the Holy One of Israel, "Since you have rejected this word And have put your trust in oppression and guile, and have relied on them..."

Jeremiah 23:16-17 *Thus says the Lord of hosts, "Do not listen to the words of the prophets who are prophesying to you. They are leading you into futility; They speak a vision of their own imagination, Not from the mouth of the Lord. They keep saying to those who despise Me, 'The Lord has said, "You will have peace" '; And as for everyone who walks in the stubbornness of his own heart, They say, 'Calamity will not come upon you.'"*

One thing you can count on with a true prophet is that he will not always say everything is okay. Therefore, how do we reconcile this with I Corinthians 14:3? Look at the wording. *"One who prophesies speaks to men for edification, and exhortation, and consolation."* The use of the word "for" means that the result of prophecy is for edification, exhortation, and consolation. That does not mean that the message is going to be words **of** edification, exhortation, and consolation.

For instance, if a prophet gives me a word of correction and I hear it and repent, the results of that are edification, exhortation, and consolation. The edification, exhortation, and consolation are the results of the prophetic word not the prophetic words. The New Testament prophet is no different than the Old Testament prophet, but the New Testament environment in which prophets minister has changed drastically. Whereas previously only the prophets and kings were indwelled with the Spirit of God, now all believers are indwelled with the Spirit of God.

> *Acts 2:15-17 "For these men are not drunk, as you suppose, for it is only the third hour of the day; but this is what was spoken of through the prophet Joel: 'And it shall be in the last days,' God says, 'That I will pour forth of My Spirit on all mankind; And your sons and your daughters shall prophesy, And your young men shall see visions, And your old men shall dream dreams...'"*

As with all the offices of ministry, prophets cannot just "turn off" the gift; they are operating in it all the time. For most callings this is not a problem necessarily, but for the prophet it is a continuous source of trouble. Why? The gifting of being in the prophetic gift all the time causes prophets to see things in the future all the time. At first this may sound completely daffy. Let me explain.

When a prophet sees the destiny upon a person, it causes the prophet to treat that person in the context of his call. Therefore, when a prophet sees that person engage in a conduct that is damaging to the prophetic future, the prophet reacts according to the prophetic future and not the current circumstances. Thus, the prophet's response may be seen as over-reacting, but in the context of that person's future, it is not.

I learned much of this through being married to a prophetess. Early in our marriage I could not determine when she was prophesying or when she was just talking. I have noticed that often time prophets don't even know they are prophesying. This is born out in Scripture as well. King David was also a prophet. Look at the wording of his prophecy concerning Judas' betrayal of Jesus.

Psalm 41:9 *Even my close friend in whom I trusted, Who ate my bread, Has lifted up his heel against me.*

This was a Messianic psalm prophesying the betrayal of Judas, yet when you read that verse in the context of the chapter, David was complaining about those who had taken advantage of him. At one point David even admitted to sinning, so this passage cannot be all about Jesus, since Jesus never sinned. I think this is just an example of how the prophetic often works when one walks in the office of prophet.

I will give you some examples from my own experience. After studying the prophetic ministry in my wife, I began to learn some things that clued me in concerning when she was prophesying. For instance, we were in the process of purchasing a new home. Having come from the bank after learning that we were approved for the loan, my wife excitedly began to call her relatives.

When her relatives asked her what the interest rate was, she replied, *"It's six and a half percent."* I would correct her on the phone and say, *"No, it is seven percent."* She called another relative and she said six and a half percent again. I corrected her again, and this happened about four times. It was at that point I realized that she was seeing in the future and was prophesying the interest rate that we would be able to lock in on.

About a month later we were in the parking lot of a shopping center and the realtor who sold us the home happened to be in the same parking lot. When he saw us he came over to greet us. Then he asked if we had locked in on an interest rate yet. I immediately spoke up and said, *"No, I am holding out for six and a half percent."* The realtor took out his phone and called my bank and asked to speak to the loan officer.

When the loan officer came to the phone, the realtor told her that we wanted to lock in on a rate of six and a half percent. She began checking the rates and then told him that they just dropped to six and a half percent. We asked if we needed to come to the bank to lock in the rate and she said that all she needed was a verbal agreement over the phone. So we locked in at six and a half percent! The prophecy had been fulfilled. My wife looked more shocked than I did. By the time we closed on our house the rate had climbed again to seven percent.

This was the beginning of dozens of such events. The problem, though, is that there are many people who do not understand that a person is a prophet and misinterpret their actions toward them. Prophets are often written off as strange or indifferent. This is far from the truth; they are just as normal as the rest of us. The problem is that they are seeing a different picture then the rest of us.

We are living in the here and now; they are living in the future, yet they often think they are seeing in the present. This causes a disconnect in the perception of the present and a communication that is based upon the future. This is why prophets can often times become reclusive as a result of the treatment that they receive from others, especially family members who know them best.

A good example of this is an event that took place shortly after the 9/11 attacks in New York. We were in the process of moving to our new home and needed some help. My wife's brother was going to help, but we needed one more person. She very emphatically commanded that we invite a young man named Brandon to help us. She would not take no for an answer.

We invited him to help and he did. I realized that this young man was a substance abuser. When I took him to lunch I said, *"Brandon, God has more for your life than this."* I had no idea the impact those words had. After the move we received a call from him telling us he had checked himself into detox and wanted us to be his pastors. We accepted and ministered to him when he left detox and entered the halfway house system.

When it came time for him to leave the halfway house my wife said that we needed to take him into our home else he would be around other drug addicts and get pulled back in to that life. I agreed so we brought Brandon to our home. We had a wonderful time ministering to him. He was so hungry to learn of God and we could hardly feed him the Word fast enough.

One day as we were sitting at our kitchen table, Brandon pulled out a picture to show us that was taken of him the very day he went into detox. When my wife saw the picture she was visibly upset and confused. She asked me, *"Is this the man we let into our house?"* I answered in the affirmative. She said, *"That is not the Brandon I saw. I saw the Brandon as he looks now."* It was then that she realized she was seeing him prophetically as he would be, not as he was. She looked at that picture again and said, *"I would never have let that man into my house."*

The important part of this story is not what my wife was seeing, but that a young man addicted to drugs was miraculously set free because of the prophetic direction given. This underscores the need for this ministry in the Church. This so upset my wife that she wondered if she were actually seeing people accurately in the present.

I have learned to lean very safely upon the prophetic gift in my wife. I have never seen it fail. I, however, am very anchored to the present and this can cause much upheaval with a mate who is walking in the office of the prophet. We can be looking at the same thing, yet my perception of it is tied to the present and her perception of it is tied to the future. Thus, two very different reactions can result.

The prophet casts the vision of the Church both individually and corporately. God divinely gives prophets the direction in which they both should begin to walk. As a visionary, prophets are careful to protect the vision of the Church even at the expense of losing people from the group. They are careful to protect the vision of the individual even at the expense of losing a friend. When we understand that the prophet can see things that we cannot, it will cause us to be understanding when communication seems to not be making sense in the present.

In discussing what prophets do, I think it is important to discuss what they don't do. I only raise this point because of some of the abuses that take place from those who proclaim to be prophetic, and may very well be prophetic, but are instead operating in witchcraft and divination. Prophets do not control people or organizations. They counsel them as to the direction in which God is calling them. They may get irritated when the vision is not followed, but that is just the passion of the call.

Prophets do not prophesy minutia. That is, they do not get involved in every aspect of a person's life. God does not want dependency upon any one minister. There are people who will not do anything without consulting a prophet. God desires His people to inquire of Him concerning all the decisions of a person's life. We are to be reliant upon God for direction. In fact, I believe that in the New Testament environment the prophetic ministry will confirm what the Holy Spirit is already communicating to that person.

1 Corinthians 12:28 And God has appointed in the Church, first apostles, second prophets, third

teachers, then miracles, then gifts of healings,
helps, administrations, various kinds of tongues.

As it concerns the Church, the prophet is needed after the apostle surveys the land and begins to build. The prophet will reveal God's vision for that church in that region. Without a vision the Church will be directionless. Prophets also assist the apostle in the revelation of gifts in individuals so that they can be set in the Church to maximize their abilities. Also, as individual destinies are revealed, each individual will begin to congeal with the group to begin their journey toward the work fashioned by God for them to accomplish.

Differences

As with most of the callings, there are a variety of differences between prophets. You can have prophets who are called to minister to heads of state, prophets who are counselors, prophets called to minister to nations, etc. Nevertheless, we must not lose sight of the fact that they are all equippers. This means that they also teach the Word of God.

Pluck Up, Break Down, Build, and Plant

> **Jeremiah 1:10** *"See, I have appointed you this day over the nations and over the kingdoms, To pluck up and to break down, To destroy and to overthrow, To build and to plant."*

Jeremiah was called to be a prophet. Not every prophet is the same. There are many nuances that show differences in each one. In this case the prophet was to destroy and overthrow, then they were to build and plant. Much of what stands in the way of destiny the prophets will address in a person's life. This means that there must be some tearing down and some overthrowing in order to set that person in the place where the prophet can begin to speak destiny to build and plant.

Another interesting point is that nations are the Hebrew *goy* and specifically dealing with any nation but Israel. The word for gentiles comes from this. The Hebrews call them *goyim.* The word for kingdoms, however, can be any domain with a king, even a spiritual kingdom.

Contend With the Forces of Darkness.

> *1 Kings 18:19 "Now then send and gather to me all Israel at Mount Carmel, together with 450 prophets of Baal and 400 prophets of the Asherah, who eat at Jezebel's table."*

One godly prophet commanded a showdown on Mt. Carmel; eight hundred and fifty prophets of Baal against one prophet of God. We know what happened; God showed up and those wicked prophets were slain. In this we see that real prophets are troubled by false prophets and will call them out with great ferocity.

When my wife had a death experience a few years ago, she was walking down an amber lit path with darkness on both sides. She began looking at the darkness and started seeing silhouettes moving in the dark. As she got closer she noticed demonic leaders quoting Scriptures with a twisted meaning attached to them. She looked at them and pointed and said, *"That's not right!"* You can read the rest of this story in our book on spiritual warfare. I wanted to share this to show that prophets are constantly on the watch for forces of darkness trying to stop the will of God in the earth.

> ***Zechariah 1:4*** *"Do not be like your fathers, to whom the former prophets proclaimed, saying, 'Thus says the LORD of hosts, "Return now from your evil ways and from your evil deeds."' But they did not listen or give heed to Me," declares the LORD.*

Prophets call people to return from their wicked ways to walk in the ways of God. You can scarcely hear this rebuke coming from the prophetic ministry today. There is a type of political correctness that has hindered the operation of the prophetic with regard to correction and rebuke. Prophets will cry out against the sins of the people. Why? Because of their passion for the destiny of a person or a people, they see the end result of sin and its devastating effects upon the destiny of a person or people.

Proclaim Judgments to Come Upon People and Nations

> ***Jonah 3:4*** *Then Jonah began to go through the city one day's walk; and he cried out and said, "Yet forty days and Nineveh will be overthrown."*

Jonah proclaimed God's judgment upon the Ninevites. Nineveh was spared because the leadership and the people repented. Had they not, God would have destroyed that city. The prophet is called to make these proclamations.

Proclaim Natural Disasters

> ***Acts 11:27-28*** *Now at this time some prophets came down from Jerusalem to Antioch. One of them named Agabus stood up and began to indicate by the Spirit that there would certainly be a great*

famine all over the world. And this took place in the reign of Claudius.

Here again is something that many prophetic schools teach prophets not to do. How can this be? God has given us the prophet to warn us so that we can prepare. God does not want His people in the dark regarding the future.

Amos 3:7 *Surely the Lord GOD does nothing Unless He reveals His secret counsel To His servants the prophets.*

How Would I Recognize This Call In Myself or Others?

The prophet has a passion for the vision. When that vision is in danger the prophet reacts now according to what they see in the future. An individual who is turning down a particular road, which to those of us who are not prophets may seem innocuous, yet in reality is causing a destruction of that person's destiny, causes the prophet to react as if that road is the most dangerous thing to pursue. It may not make sense to the rest of us; nevertheless, the prophet's counsel should be heeded.

You need to think of a prophet's actions as *end–result* oriented. If you could see the end of something based upon a decision made today, you certainly would react differently than you would without that information. I am completely intrigued by the prophetic ministry. I stand amazed as I watch them in their call.

What are the Prophet's Gifts?

The prophet obviously operates in the gift of **prophecy**. Also, the prophet often operates in the gift of **discernment**. I think that those two gifts are almost inseparable in the prophetic office. If the prophet sees the destiny of a person, then the prophet will often see the intent of that person now. Jesus walked in the prophetic gifting and knew that Judas would betray Him. It is interesting that at the last supper Jesus plainly tells the twelve that one of them would betray Him. Moreover, they were clueless as to whom that could be, questioning themselves and asking the Master if it were them. Another gift that the prophet usually walks in is the **word of knowledge**. This is evidenced by the revelation of the human heart.

> *1 Corinthians 14:24-25 But if all prophesy, and an unbeliever or an ungifted man enters, he is convicted by all, he is called to account by all; the secrets of his heart are disclosed; and so he will fall on his face and worship God, declaring that God is certainly among you.*

Here we see the association of prophecy and the gift of the word of knowledge. They also often operate in the **gift of exhortation**.

What is the Prophetic Church?

The prophetic church will be a place where the prophetic ministry is welcomed and encouraged. It is also a church that is highly focused in the vision that is prophetically cast for it. That church will be known for bringing the prophetic into every part of ministry. There will be prophetic teaching, vision, dreams, prophetic evangelism, etc.

Summation

This office is both the most intriguing, and at the same time, the most complex to understand. All the same, it reaps some of the greatest rewards. There can be no mistake; God has ordained prophets in the Church to facilitate the equipping of the saints through the revelation of their call and destiny and by constantly monitoring that call so that time is never wasted in getting to it. I think back upon my own life and wonder what the difference would be if I had been exposed to more true prophetic ministry. I am sure there would be times of rebuke, encouragement, counsel, and revelation.

I cannot leave this subject without speaking to any ministers that might be reading this. Many ministers have given up allowing prophets access to their congregations. This is unfortunate, but I understand your desire to protect your sheep. Yes, there are some false ones out there just as there are false pastors and teachers. We need to take Apostle Paul's admonition to heart.

> *1 Thessalonians 5:20-22 do not despise prophetic utterances. But examine everything carefully; hold fast to that which is good; abstain from every form of evil.*

Apparently, Paul saw some problems in his day as well, but he did not dismiss this calling. Instead, he admonished us to examine everything carefully. I have found it helpful to have a meeting with those who received a prophetic utterance and examine it with them. Sometimes the person would not think that a prophetic word belonged to them, yet on closer inspection they were relieved. Sometimes it went the other way. But what is important is that we are not to despise any of the gifts given by the Holy Spirit to the Church.

The Teacher

he office of the ministry would surely not be complete
without this calling. Its gifts and passions are such that it
keeps the Body of Christ on track when it goes astray in
doctrine. We are talking about the teacher.

What is a Teacher?

When looking at the Hebrew words that are translated into
"teacher," it is interesting to note the two main words and their
definitions.

> DEFINITION
>
> *3384 [yarah, Chr., yara' /yaw·raw/] v. A
> primitive root; 1 to throw, shoot, cast, pour. 1a
> (Qal). 1a1 to throw, cast. 1a2 to cast, lay, set.
> 1a3 to shoot arrows. 1a4 to throw water, rain. 1b
> (Niphal) to be shot. 1c (Hiphil). 1c1 to throw,
> cast. 1c2 to shoot. 1c3 to point out, show. 1c4 to
> direct, teach, instruct. 1c5 to throw water, rain.*
>
> *4175 [mowreh /mo·reh/] n m. From 3384; TWOT
> 910b, 910c; GK 4619 and 4620 and 4621; Three
> occurrences; AV translates as "former rain"
> twice, and "rain" once. 1 (early) rain. 2 (TWOT)
> teacher.* [24]

---

[24] *(Strong, J., 1996)*

Remember that Hebrew is a pictorial language. I find it very telling that rain is associated with being a teacher. In order to understand the significance of this we need to take a look at a certain parable taught by the Master, Jesus.

> *Luke 8:9-15 His disciples began questioning Him as to what this parable meant. And He said, "To you it has been granted to know the mysteries of the kingdom of God, but to the rest it is in parables, so that seeing they may not see, and hearing they may not understand."*
>
> *Now the parable they are questioning Jesus about is this: the seed is the word of God. Those beside the road are those who have heard; then the devil comes and takes away the word from their heart, so that they will not believe and be saved.*
>
> *Those on the rocky soil are those who, when they hear, receive the word with joy; and these have no firm root; they believe for a while, and in time of temptation fall away.*
>
> *The seed which fell among the thorns, these are the ones who have heard, and as they go on their way they are choked with worries and riches and pleasures of this life, and bring no fruit to maturity.*
>
> *But the seed in the good soil, these are the ones who have heard the word in an honest and good heart, and hold it fast, and bear fruit with perseverance.*

The Word of God is pictured by Jesus as a seed. In order to understand the role of a teacher, we need to understand what effect the teacher can have upon the seed, or the Word of God. In the desert where there can be years at a time without rain, something wonderful happens when it finally rains. Plant life begins to sprout and grow out of the ground, and suddenly, that which was a dry, dead, and barren land is bringing forth life.

This is why the teacher is so connected to rain in the Hebrew language. Just as a seed without water is unable to grow, so the Christian, who may have the seed of the Word of God but without understanding, cannot grow. Thus, the primary role of the teacher to the Church is to bring understanding concerning the Word of God that it may produce growth in the Body of Christ. This is for what a teacher will live and strive; to bring understanding.

Some of you may ask at this point, *"What about the Hebrew word, Rabbi, which is used in the New Testament as the title for teacher?"* If that question has been raised in your mind, you are to be commended. Here is the Scripture that brings this question to mind.

> **John 1:38** *And Jesus turned and saw them following, and said to them, "What do you seek?" They said to Him, "Rabbi (which translated means Teacher), where are You staying?"*

Interestingly, this Hebrew word is not translated *"teacher"* in the Hebrew Scriptures. It is translated as great, master, multiply, archer, shot, etc. What is significant is that it agrees with the Hebrew words already given earlier in this chapter.

What Does a Teacher Do?

The teacher loves the Word and studies diligently. The teacher will study words and their meanings. The teacher will relentlessly look for the original intent of the author through the meaning of words and the context in which they are found.

The teacher must do extensive research. The teacher is constantly looking for not only personal understanding, but also ways in which to make the data understandable to the audience. There is a driving force to learn that is insatiable; they read often and may keep to themselves more than most. This is all for the purpose of being able to lay out in clear and understandable terms the Word of God in order that it will be digestible by the hearers and thereby produce faith.

The teacher wants to understand all that they study. So the teacher of Scripture will want to understand all Scripture. Still, the teacher will have to be honest with oneself and admit that they do not understand all Scripture entirely. There are things that teachers don't understand, so they can't let these things misdirect their paths. Teachers like to be able to give answers to questions they are asked. It is important that teachers be willing to say, *"I don't know."* when necessary.

> **Proverbs 3:5-6** *Trust in the Lord with all your heart; do not depend on your own understanding. Seek his will in all you do, and he will direct your paths.*

I know that in my own studies this has been very rewarding. It is easy to go with the status quo and not buck the system when you see the system in error. Nevertheless, this is for what the teacher exists; they will correct and instruct in doctrine. The teacher may at times seem cold or indifferent. This is because they are focused on correct doctrine more than saving someone's feelings. This is also something of which the teacher must be careful; they must try to deliver what they know in a way that takes into account the person who they are correcting.

How Would I Recognize This Call in Myself or Others?

One thing that is recognizable in teachers is that they are skeptical but not to a fault; they just need everything supported with facts. This, again, must be tempered with the knowledge that any one teacher does not understand all things. What the teacher does understand is usually solid; it does not make leaps of assumption and subjection.

When I read a Christian author I am the most irritated when they resort to conjecture to prove a point. This is because conjecture does not prove anything; it only supposes it. I have seen many good subjects presented with good research and factual reporting diminished because the author decided to interject some conjecture to arrive at a certain point.

You will find that teachers often quote the Bible or use illustrations from the Bible rather than from other sources. The reason for this is that because they are somewhat skeptical and know there is only one reliable source of truth, they trust and rely on the Bible. One thing that many, myself included, find irritating about teachers is that they always want to be right. I have seen many of my own discussions ended with the other person accusing me of always wanting to be right.

Well, yes, I do want to be right; it would be silly to want to be wrong. Teachers tend to be dogmatic in their field of study and this can also make them seem annoying. They seem too sure of themselves at times and this appears to others as arrogance. It is not in many cases; true arrogance is placing one's self above others, but just being right does not elevate one's self above another who is wrong. The teacher's motive in being right should be to TEACH others how to be right. A teacher should teach so the student will be able to defend what they believe and have a solid reasoning for those beliefs.

Matthew 28:19-20 Therefore, go and make disciples of all the nations, baptizing them in the name of the Father and the Son and the Holy Spirit. Teach these new disciples to obey all the commands I have given you. And be sure of this: I am with you always, even to the end of the age.

This is the teacher's motivation, not to be elevated, but to elevate the student. The teacher also feels it necessary that truth be established in every situation. It is vitally important that nothing be left to chance. When I teach a lesson my goal is to impart truth. A teacher will feel it necessary to hear all sides of the argument in order that belief will be based upon solid facts, not supposition.

Teachers are more objective rather than subjective. They often look at life with a bit of detachment. They don't let their emotions get in the way of their objectivity. For this, they are many times labeled as cold or uncaring.

One theme that I have tried to continue through each calling that we study is that we are all different and we all do things differently. The more we know about the differences in the callings the easier it is to tolerate each other in our ministries. The pastor may look at the teacher and say, *"Have you no feelings?"* The teacher may look at the pastor and say, *"Have you no common sense?"* So it is important that we tolerate each other and realize that we minister according to our gifts, which are different.

The teacher says anything that is not of the truth is a lie and is dangerous. Truth is the essence of God. God is truth. Jesus said, *"I am the way, the TRUTH, and the life"* (John 14:6). Truth is vitally important to the teacher. I think that it should be vitally important to all the callings, but I think that because I am a teacher.

*1 **Timothy 1:3** When I left for Macedonia, I urged
you to stay there in Ephesus and stop those who are
teaching wrong doctrine.*

Teachers absolutely cannot tolerate wrong doctrine; it is so
offensive to them that they will speak out immediately. Remember,
this is their calling, and as such their desire is truth, or correct
doctrine. Timothy was a teacher; he was instructed by Apostle Paul
to guard his teaching.

*1 **Timothy 4:13 -16** Until I get there, focus on
reading the Scriptures to the Church, encouraging
the believers, and **teaching them**. Do not neglect
the spiritual gift you received through the
prophecies spoken to you when the elders of the
Church laid their hands on you. Give your complete
attention to these matters. Throw yourself into your
tasks so that everyone will see your progress. **Keep
a close watch on yourself and on your teaching**.
Stay true to what is right, and God will save you
and those who hear you.*

"Stay true to what is right." This is the anthem cry of the
teacher. For this he is cautious in his teaching, often desiring to run
it by others before making it public. He welcomes criticism as it
helps to polish and finalize the teaching. So, if you are ever asked
to look over an article by a teacher, be totally honest and give him
your best criticism. You may not be correct in your critique, but at
least you will be respected for giving your honest opinion of the
writing.

*2 **Timothy 2:1-2** Timothy, my dear son, be strong
with the special favor God gives you in Christ
Jesus. You have heard me teach many things that
have been confirmed by many reliable witnesses.*

***Teach these great truths to trustworthy people who
are able to pass them on to others.***

One of the greatest goals of the teacher is to enable others
to teach what they too have been taught. This calling, as all others,
is not to gain personal status, but to perpetuate the gospel of God.
It is not to lift up one's self, but to lift up others that they, too, will
lift up others. As in all callings, teachers should be humble and
realize that God gives them the wisdom and knowledge that they
have.

Notice also, that the teaching is to be passed on to
TRUSTWORTHY people. People who love God and seek to serve
in the spreading of the Good News are to be the recipients of
Timothy's teaching. They are to be people who will not get puffed
up with much knowledge, but will remain humble knowing that it
is the Spirit who gives them this gift.

> ***2 Timothy 2:24-26*** *The Lord's servants must not
> quarrel but must be kind to everyone. They must be
> able to teach effectively and be patient with difficult
> people.* ***They should gently teach those who oppose
> the truth.*** *Perhaps God will change those people's
> hearts, and they will believe the truth. Then they
> will come to their senses and escape from the
> Devil's trap. For they have been held captive by
> him to do whatever he wants.*

It is important to understand what the word "quarrel"
means. The Greek word is *machomai* and it has the same meaning
as hand-to-hand combat. This word is used in four places in the
New Testament. I want to look at each occurrence so you will
understand what the true meaning of this is. We have seen one of
the four references above so let's look at the other three.

*John 6:52 Then the people began **arguing** with each other about what he meant. "How can this man give us his flesh to eat?" they asked.*

This took place right after Jesus declared that He was the bread of life and those who ate of His flesh would live forever. Making this claim incensed the Jews; it was a deplorable thing to eat the flesh of another human. They were offended and began fighting about it. Therefore, we see the word here used in a sense of anger in their discussion.

*Acts 7:26 "The next day he visited them again and saw two men of Israel **fighting**. He tried to be a peacemaker. `Men,` he said, `you are brothers. Why are you hurting each other?`"*

This instance is the telling of the story of Moses when he visited his brothers and saw them fighting. Earlier he had struck down the Egyptian who was abusing his brothers. In the verse before this one, it is said that Moses supposed his brethren understood that God was granting them deliverance through him. Instead, he saw them fighting, obviously physically, for he asked, *"Why are you hurting each other?"* The response that he received is recorded in the next few verses.

Acts 7:27-29 The man who was hurting the other pushed Moses away and said, `Who made you our ruler and judge? Are you going to kill me as you killed the Egyptian yesterday?` When Moses heard him say this, he left Egypt and went to live in the land of Midian where he was a stranger. While Moses lived in Midian, he had two sons.

Here we see the evidence that there was a physical struggle since it says, *"The man who was hurting the other."* Therefore, again, we get the ideal meaning of this word as something altogether different than a civil conversation. The final instance of this word is used in James.

> **James 4:2** *You want what you don't have, so you scheme and kill to get it. You are jealous for what others have, and you can't possess it, so you fight and quarrel to take it away from them. And yet the reason you don't have what you want is that you don't ask God for it.*

This last instance has the word quarrel with it as well, but this is a different Greek word and not the same Greek word as used in Acts. It means *"to war."* Hence, we see once more that this word is not used for a civil debate; it is used for fighting, even physically. Still, many quote this verse when they see a civil debate taking place. They misuse Scripture and apply it to the wrong situation. Civil debate is a wonderful way to learn, both for those debating and for those listening or watching.

There are times when one of the debaters may become uncivil, but if the other debater is civil, then there is no reason to get upset at both parties. Nonetheless, this happens all the time. There is scolding and rebuking going to both, even though one of the debaters is civil. We must keep in mind that there will be disagreements concerning doctrine. When these disagreements occur between Christians they are often about secondary doctrinal issues. When it involves cults or atheists and agnostics, however, it is often regarding primary doctrinal issues that are serious to the faith.

> **2 Timothy 3:16-17** *All Scripture is inspired by God and is useful to teach us what is true and to make us realize what is wrong in our lives. It straightens us out and teaches us to do what is right. 17 It is God's*

way of preparing us in every way, fully equipped for
every good thing God wants us to do.

The Passion of the Teacher

Surely, teaching is the greatest gift and job in the world. The prize of teaching is **truth transferred**. It is not an easy task, but it is a noble one. This is especially true when dealing with controversial subjects. Teaching is really the art of making the complex simple, the mysterious revealed, the long interesting, the short exciting, and the random ordered and in place.

The teacher is always looking for different ways to present the same truths. A single way of presentation is not sufficient. In the teacher's quiver there must be an assortment of arrows to answer every question, every objection, and any confusion. There are many different types of students, so there must necessarily be different presentations of the same truth.

There is nothing to compare to what I like to call, "the look." It is seen at that moment when the light goes on and someone just increased their knowledge. When a person "gets it," their face lights up as if someone just turned the light on inside and now it's shining out of the windows into the dark to give light to all. At that moment the teacher receives their greatest prize. It is the satisfaction of all the hard work done that no one sees. All the hours of study and all the hours of presentation are suddenly worth it for just that one look.

Teachers many times are not appreciated, but that does not deter them. The quest of bringing a truth to another person is not a small thing. It is the unlocking of the hidden recesses of a person's life; it is the opening of doors that were closed. What you have done is to bring another slice of freedom to the person you taught. That person now possesses the freedom not to be tricked or deceived in that area ever again. That person possesses the freedom to think, speak, and act upon reality rather than perception. You have armed him with the ability to pass on that knowledge to another.

When you are called as a teacher and see that you are actually making people free, the nobility of teaching is found. It doesn't mean that others will see the nobility of teaching, but you will, and you will be satisfied knowing that you have one of the most important jobs in the world – bringing light to places that were dark and making free what was in captivity. You are a bringer of good things. Understand who you are; you are a teacher.

As I stated earlier, the teacher has an insatiable desire to learn. As such, teachers spend much of their time in study. They have a strong desire for truth and strongly dislike conjecture and subjectivity. They love the Word of God strongly, because it is the only tangible thing they have that can be called absolute truth. That is why, to the teacher, everything revolves around the Word. When others may use life illustrations, the teacher will often use biblical illustration.

Teachers obviously have a strong desire to pass on their knowledge. They love to teach. They desire to keep the Body of Christ correct in doctrine. As such, they must correct others. This is not done to belittle or defame others, but rather to uplift and strengthen them. Teachers have a passion for correct teaching. They have a passion to make their material understandable, logical, and well organized.

The Gifts of the Teacher

Obviously, they have the gift of teaching. It is important to note again that there are two gifts with the same name as the calling; they are prophecy and prophet, as well as teaching and teacher. In addition, it is important to note that the prophet and teacher each protect the Body of Christ in different aspects; the prophet from lack of vision and the teacher from lack of truth. This is the only obvious spiritual gift in the teacher. It does not mean that it is the only gift a teacher has for the Spirit gives gifts as He wills. Remember not to look at this list as all-inclusive.

The Teaching Church

The church that accepts the calling of a teacher will become a teaching church. The result is that there will be a congregation that is able to defend outside the church what they believe to be true inside the church. They will be aware of the latest fads of false teachings. The Body of Christ will have a depth of knowledge concerning the doctrines of our faith. This will result in a congregation that is consistently taking what they are learning and making it a part of their life, producing a walk that is worthy of the Lord. They will also be aware of the different cults that are impacting the current culture. Since the call of teacher is one of the most dangerous, there is a clear warning in Scripture for the teacher.

> *James 3:1 Dear brothers and sisters, not many of you should become teachers in the Church, for we who teach will be judged by God with greater strictness.*

James reveals that God will judge teachers with a greater harshness than others are judged. Teaching is not something to be entered into frivolously. Take with great seriousness the call to be a teacher.

Summation

If you are called to be a teacher you should see some of these characteristics in yourself. You will find your reward in the learning of others. It is so rewarding that you want to do it over and over. One caution, though, is not to let it rule your life. You still need to be a human to your family and friends, and you need to be a minister to the hurting as well. It is important for the minister to balance his life.

Too much ministering will burn you out and you will be neglecting other important areas in your life. I can only say that it has been an absolute joy to be a teacher. Again, remember that God calls you. He plants the desire in you to fulfill that calling, and He equips you with the gifts to operate in that calling. At any rate, incumbent upon the teacher is the responsibility to increase in the knowledge of God and that takes much study and research.

The Pastor

Chapter Nine

We have now taken a look at the apostle, prophet, and teacher. Next, we are going to discuss another office of the five fold ministry. This calling is the one that is the most popular and widely accepted amongst protestant organizations. It is for this reason that the word "pastor" has become a generic term for any minister regardless to which office they are called.

What is a Pastor?

The word "pastor" in the Greek is the same as shepherd. In fact, that Greek word is translated 17 of the 18 times as shepherd in the King James Version. There is only one instance of "pastor." The word is from the Latin *pãstor* which means shepherd. They are literally interchangeable, so I will use the word pastor, since that is the most common and more easily identified.

Since this calling is that of a common word, shepherd, then we can look at what this word leads to and get a better idea of this calling. The shepherd was a tender of sheep. If we look at this occupation we get a good insight as to what the pastor's calling looks like.

There is a very good book available that shows this relationship. It is called *"A Shepherd's Look at the 23rd Psalm"* and is authored by Phillip W. Keller. Although it is out of print you should be able to find it somewhere; it may even be in your local library.

7462 [ra`ah /raw·aw/] v. A primitive root; TWOT 1 to pasture, tend, graze, feed. 1a (Qal). 1a1 to tend, pasture. 1a1a to shepherd. 1a1b of ruler, teacher (fig). 1a1c of people as flock (fig). 1a1d shepherd, herdsman (subst). 1a2 to feed, graze. 1a2a of cows, sheep etc (literal). 1a2b of idolater, Israel as flock (fig). 1b (Hiphil) shepherd, shepherdess. 2 to associate with, be a friend of (meaning probable). 2a (Qal) to associate with. 2b (Hithpael) to be companions. 3 (Piel) to be a special friend.[25]

The picture this Hebrew word paints is very endearing. I want to bring special attention to the third definition in which the Piel sense of the verb is rendered as, *"to be a special friend."* This really does show the call and passion of the pastor.

What Does a Pastor Do?

The pastor's relationship to the Body of Christ is one of endearing care. It is a strenuous calling and requires patience, mercy, and a deep sense of love for the people of God. The pastor will exhibit a protective spirit over those he is tending. This protection is not just from outsiders, but from sickness and emotional pain as well. This responsibility allows pastors to be able to sense a troubled spirit and emotional distress of one of their flock.

As a shepherd leads his flock, a pastor will lead the people in his care. Sometimes sheep don't understand all the danger that

---

[25] - *(Strong, J., 1996)*

they can get themselves into; the same is true of many Christians. The pastor will watch over the flock to make sure they are kept safe.

This is the sense that we get from David's psalm, *"The Lord is my Shepherd, I shall not want"* (Psalm 23:1). The pastor will look to the wellness of his flock and that goes in many different directions. He looks to all the needs of those in his care.

Can we say that this is just spiritual application and not actual, physical needs? No!! Jesus Himself said, *"I was thirsty and you did not give me drink, I was hungry and you did not feed me, I was naked and you did not clothe me, I was in prison and you did not visit me, I was sick and you did not care for me"* (Matthew 25). You see the need from this that God is not only concerned with the spiritual, but the physical as well.

It is not only the pastor that feeds the sheep: all of the five callings do this, but there is a special care involved with the pastor. Although it is not always the case, the apostle, prophet, evangelist, and even the teacher can all be traveling ministries and as such their concern can be for a number of local churches. The pastor, on the other hand, is local, and his concern is primarily for the local body. Even the kings were seen as shepherd over the nation of Israel.

> *1 Chronicles 11:2 "In times past, even when Saul was king, you were the one who led out and brought in Israel; and the LORD your God said to you, 'You shall shepherd My people Israel, and you shall be prince over My people Israel.'"*

This was being said of David. Of course, David was a shepherd of sheep when the prophet Samuel anointed him to be the king of Israel. What needs to be understood about this calling is that it is not just about leadership. The sheep are loved by the shepherd and they receive protection, care, food, correction, and direction from him. Remember that God is our shepherd and He leads us to still waters. I know that congregations want to think they are mature and able to handle themselves by themselves. Nevertheless, God gave this gift to the Church to watch over His flock.

How many people really don't want a person to watch over them? How many congregations set their own policies? How many congregations choose their own shepherds and then fire them when they attempt to correct them? I hope that these few questions will cause you to think about how out of order it is for congregants to have that kind of authority over their pastors. The government of God is not negotiable. He decides how He rules and whom He rules through.

> *Isaiah 40:11* *Like a shepherd He will tend His flock, In His arm He will gather the lambs And carry them in His bosom; He will gently lead the nursing ewes.*

Shepherds will give more or special attention to the weaker ones in the group; to those that are helpless, burdened, or weighed down. One only needs to think of Jesus when He talked about leaving the ninety-nine to go after the one that went astray.

Shepherds feed their flock with knowledge and understanding. They lead them to the water of the Word and to the living waters of the Holy Spirit. Not everyone who says they are a pastor actually is functioning like one. Yes, there will be those who are in it for themselves. This is not the case for the real shepherd. His joy is a healthy well fed and well watered flock.

Jeremiah 23:4 *"I will also raise up shepherds over them and they will tend them; and they will not be afraid any longer, nor be terrified, nor will any be missing," declares the* LORD.

Shepherds will have the ability to remove fear from the flock. There is no other calling that this can be said of with regard to anointing. This is why pastors often have the gift of exhortation. They motivate and give the sheep hope when they are having life problems. Imagine being sheep in the midst of terror and at the same time having no fear of it. This is the blessing that the pastor can bring to a congregation.

Pastors will also have an anointing to keep the sheep in the fold. How many groups who have no pastor have problems keeping the sheep? Oh, that God would send us pastors to tend the sheep.

Jeremiah 33:12 *"Thus says the* LORD *of hosts, 'There will again be in this place which is waste, without man or beast, and in all its cities, a habitation of shepherds who rest their flocks.'"*

Rest is another quality the pastor will bring to his people. Rest is also the manifestation of peace. It shows that the enemies are at a safe distance away from the flock. The flock needs rest in order to flourish and prosper.

Ezekiel chapter thirty-four offers a stern warning against the bad shepherd. When we read it we are faced with things that the shepherds did not do. By looking at their failure we can deduce success.

Ezekiel 34:2 *"Son of man, prophesy against the shepherds of Israel. Prophesy and say to those shepherds, 'Thus says the Lord* GOD, *"Woe, shepherds of Israel who have been feeding themselves! Should not the shepherds feed the flock?*

When I read this verse I think of all of the church organizations who do not disciple their congregants. I think about shepherds who continue to learn themselves, but they are not equipping their members. Notice what happens when the sheep are not fed.

Ezekiel 34:3 *"You eat the fat and clothe yourselves with the wool, you slaughter the fat sheep without feeding the flock."*

What would this mean? There are ministers who only seek what they can get from the sheep without regard to giving anything to them. These take and take, but they do not feed the flock.

Ezekiel 34:4 *"Those who are sickly you have not strengthened, the diseased you have not healed, the broken you have not bound up, the scattered you have not brought back, nor have you sought for the lost; but with force and with severity you have dominated them."*

Apparently, the shepherd is responsible to bring healing to the sheep; not only physical but emotional, as well. Remember when Jesus quoted from Isaiah by saying that He had come to bind up the brokenhearted. This is pictured as well in this verse. These bad shepherds also did not seek the lost. I think this refers to those sheep or Christians that have gone astray. They need to hunt for them and seek to restore them to the flock.

Ezekiel 34:5 *"They were scattered for lack of a shepherd, and they became food for every beast of the field and were scattered.*

What is the result of these bad shepherds? The sheep become a prey for the beast of the field. Although the beast of the field could be any group of animals that feed on sheep, one in particular comes to mind. The Bible tells us that Satan roams around like a roaring lion seeking whom he can devour. That means that he cannot just devour anyone, only those who are weak and left without a shepherd to protect them.

We need to make sure that as pentecostal and charismatic churches that we do not dismiss this calling in the church. It will bring a blessing to the group when allowed to operate in the power and anointing that our Lord has given it.

> *Matthew 9:35-38 Jesus traveled through all the cities and villages of that area, teaching in the synagogues and announcing the Good News about the Kingdom. And wherever he went, he healed people of every sort of disease and illness. He felt great pity for the crowds that came, because their problems were so great and they didn't know where to go for help. They were like sheep without a shepherd. He said to his disciples, "The harvest is so great, but the workers are so few. So pray to the Lord who is in charge of the harvest; ask him to send out more workers for his fields."*

What are these workers to do? They are to do the same thing Jesus was doing. This is not just for the pastor but for all of the callings. These poor folks were like sheep without a shepherd. What would they be like if they had a shepherd?

> *Mark 6:30-34 The apostles returned to Jesus from their ministry tour and told him all they had done and what they had taught. Then Jesus said, "Let's get away from the crowds for a while and rest."*

There were so many people coming and going that
Jesus and his apostles didn't even have time to eat.
They left by boat for a quieter spot. But many
people saw them leaving, and people from many
towns ran ahead along the shore and met them as
they landed. A vast crowd was there as he stepped
from the boat, and he had compassion on them
because they were like sheep without a shepherd. So
he taught them many things.

This passage of Scripture shows us many things. One observation is that the people recognized Jesus had the anointing on His life. One might say, *"Well, sure, but look at all the miracles He did."* Yet, we can see here that this is not why they were following Him. They were following Him to hear His teachings. That is what He did when He saw them following Him. He taught them many things.

When Jesus noticed they were like sheep without a shepherd His response was one of compassion, and the result of that compassion was that He became a shepherd to them and taught them many things. Jesus desired to help them, not only physically, but also spiritually. He wanted to give them comfort. He wanted them to be satisfied. This is the call of a shepherd.

I want to reiterate something here: one calling is not greater than another calling. The pastor is not greater than the apostle and the teacher is not greater than the prophet. I don't want anyone to think this. I have always said that the reward for obedience is the same. It does not matter to what calling the obedience is, just that we are obedient. Many times there is more than one calling in a single life. I see this all the time and there is scriptural evidence to support this, as well.

1 Timothy 2:7 And I have been chosen—this is the absolute truth—as a preacher and apostle to teach the Gentiles about faith and truth.

2 Timothy 1:10-11 And now he has made all of this plain to us by the coming of Christ Jesus, our Savior, who broke the power of death and showed us the way to everlasting life through the Good News. And God chose me to be a preacher, an apostle, and a teacher of this Good News.

I have often seen ministers that are called in this way. It would seem that they have a major and minor calling. The pastor will prefer life illustration to biblical illustration. This is not to say that he doesn't use biblical illustration. A pastor will usually feel that the application of life illustration is a great tool in their ministry, and it is.

Some may think there is very little difference between a pastor and a teacher, but there is a significant difference. The pastor's focus is on the group as a whole. The teacher's focus is on the application, discovery, and delivery of truth.

The Passions of a Pastor

- A pastor desires to lead a group and be part of that group at all times.
- A pastor will want to be responsible for the group's spiritual growth.
- A pastor will be very empathetic toward those in that group, not only for spiritual problems, but for emotional and physical problems as well.
- A pastor will desire to guard this group from the enemy, both without and within.

- A pastor will be fiercely opposed to someone trying to draw anyone from the group away into apostasy.
- A pastor will desire to present this group to Christ as a chaste virgin, a bride without spot or wrinkle.
- A pastor will desire to feed this group, to provide for their spiritual learning.
- A pastor will take great pleasure in the spiritual peace and contentment of the group.
- A truly great pastor will even give his life, as Christ did, for the group.
- A pastor is affectionate and compassionate to the group.

How Would I Recognize This Calling in Myself or Another?

It would definitely start with empathy for God's people. It is important that we don't lose sight of the fact that every calling is a gift from God. Just because we may personally see some evidences of a calling, it does not mean that the calling is there. It must be recognized by leadership that you are called.

Another sign is the desire to bring God's people together under one roof. A pastor would have a deep irritation for divisions and schisms. In addition, a pastor will usually have a desire to meet people's basic needs and may bring people off the street to give them a place to stay; whereas, the rest of us would not dare do such a thing. A pastor's empathy will sometimes even put him and others in danger.

The Gifts of the Pastor

A pastor will most probably have the gift of mercy because of their empathetic nature. Some pastors have the gift of teaching and other pastors have the gift of preaching. Many pastors have the gift of counsel and they have to deal with the emotional needs of the Church. As with the other callings, this list is not meant to be all-inclusive; nor is it meant to be a foregone conclusion.

What Does the Pastoral Church Look Like?

The pastoral church is an empathetic church. Due to its empathy for others, it will have outreach programs to help the needy. It will focus on meeting basic physical needs of life. The pastoral church feels the needs of the community and will step up to meet those needs as best as it can.

In addition to caring for the physical needs of the community, the pastoral church will care for the emotional needs, as well. Its involvement with the community will often consist of one or more programs that address those needs, such as help for alcoholics and drug addicts, single mother support, battered women shelters, and the like. This is the call of Jesus to meet the basic needs of human life and the pastoral church feels the beat of God's heart toward this endeavor.

Summation

There is an interesting Scripture in 1 Corinthians that describes something that I would like to convey at this point.

> *1 Corinthians 12:4-6 Now there are varieties of gifts, but the same Spirit. And there are varieties of ministries, and the same Lord. And there are varieties of effects, but the same God who works all things in all persons.*

This is interesting because the complete Godhead is mentioned along with the description of what He does for and in us. First, there are a variety of gifts, but the same Spirit (God the Holy Spirit) distributes these gifts as He wills. Then, there are different ministries (apostles, prophets, teachers, pastors, and evangelists), but the same Lord (God the Son) calls people to these ministries. Finally, there are a variety of effects (different combinations of gifts and callings), but the same God (God the Father) works all things in all persons.

As you can see, we have an exciting empowerment from God to fulfill our destiny on this earth. God is the One, not myself, Who determines to what I am called and with what I am gifted. I can't just wake up one day and say that I want to be an apostle. I can't just reach out and grab whatever calling I want. We are all made for a purpose and that purpose was determined before we were formed. It is up to God to perform this in you; it is up to you to submit to Him so that He may complete every good work in you.

The Evangelist

Chapter Ten

When I settled myself to begin this chapter on the evangelist I thought, *"There is not very much biblical information on this calling."* The word *"evangelist"* is only found three times in the New Testament. Compare that with seventy-seven times for the apostle, one hundred and fifty-nine for the prophet, sixty-three times for the teacher, and twenty-four times for the shepherd or pastor. Three references is not much to work from. How am I ever going to be able to do this office and calling justice? Be that as it may, when I began looking at the word in the original languages I found some surprising information.

What is an Evangelist?

Rather than starting with the Hebrew on this word as I am oft to do, we need to work backwards and start with the Greek. The reason for this is because our pronunciation is of the Greek origin.

DEFINITION

English

e-van-gel (i-vanjl)n. 1. The Christian gospel. 2. An evangelist.[Middle English evaungel, from Late Latin evangelium, from Greek euangelion, good news, from euangelos, bringing good news : eu-, eu- + angelos, messenger.] (American Heritage Dictionary, 1997)

From the etymology of this word we find the true meaning. The word is a compound of the Greek prefix *"eu"* which means *"good"* or *"good news,"* and *"angelos"* which means *"messenger."* It is a person who is a herald of good news. The word *"gospel"* means *"good news."* I found this interesting and looked up the two words in Greek to see what I would find. Here is the result:

DEFINITION

Greek

2098 [euaggelion /yoo·ang·ghel·ee·on/] 1 a reward for good tidings.

2 good tidings. 2a the glad tidings of the kingdom of God soon to be set up, and subsequently also of Jesus the Messiah, the founder of this kingdom. After the death of Christ, the term comprises also the preaching of (concerning) Jesus Christ as having suffered death on the cross to procure eternal salvation for the men in the kingdom of God, but as restored to life and exalted to the right hand of God in heaven, thence to return in majesty to consummate the kingdom of God. 2b the glad tidings of salvation through Christ. 2c the proclamation of the grace of God manifest and pledged in Christ. 2d the gospel. 2e as the messianic rank of Jesus was proved by his words, his deeds, and his death, the narrative of the sayings, deeds, and death of Jesus Christ came to be called the gospel or glad tidings. [26]

---

[26] *– (Strong, J., 1996)*

This word sounds familiar doesn't it? Yoo.angel.ee.on is very close to evangelist. This is the word that is translated *"gospel"* in the Bible. As you know, gospel means good news. So what is the connection to the evangelist? Let's look at the Greek word for *"evangelist."*

2099 *[euaggelistes /yoo·ang·ghel·is·**tace**/] **1** a bringer of good tidings, an evangelist. **2** the name given to the NT heralds of salvation through Christ who are not apostles.* [27]

Yoo.angel.is.tace is our evangelist. It is one who is a preacher of the good news of the kingdom of God. *"Word Pictures in the New Testament"* puts it this way – **"gospelizer."** Here we need to move to the Old Testament. Even though there are no instances of *"evangelist"* in the Septuagint, the word for *"gospel"* is. Looking at this word will shed some more light on the evangelist.

1319 *[basar /baw·**sar**/] v. A primitive root; **1** to bear news, bear tidings, publish, preach, show forth. **1a** (Piel). **1a1** to gladden with good news. **1a2** to bear news. **1a3** to announce (salvation) as good news, preach. **1b** (Hithpael) to receive good news.* [28]

not used in Kal; Arab. بَشِرَ *to be joyful, cheerful, especially in receiving glad tidings; Med. A. and*

---

[27] – *(Strong, J., 1996)*

[28] – *(Strong, J., 1996)*

*Conj. II. to gladden with good tidings, with an
acc. of person and ـب of thing. The primary sense
appears to be that of beauty, whence بَشِير fair,
beautiful, since a face is made more beautiful by
joy and cheerfulness (see טוֹב good, fair, joyful);
and, on the contrary, the face of a cross and
angry person is disfigured; hence بَشَرَة, يَبْشُر the
external skin of man, flesh, in which a person's
beauty is perceived.* [29]

Since Hebrew is a pictorial language it does us well to
understand the picture depicted here. The word for *"gospel"* has as
its primary sense that of *"beauty."* Why beauty? It is the result of
salvation. Kathryn and I have seen this. You will find a person who
has had a rough life and when they get saved, even their facial
features change. The good news of Jesus indeed makes one more
beautiful inwardly as they receive the peace of God that comes
with faith in Christ. When that peace is demonstrated outwardly,
the face changes.

As the Savior was born there were angelic evangelists who
proclaimed the good news of His birth. We have often put the
emphasis on saving souls concerning the evangelists, but the real
emphasis is on preaching the good news. Souls are just the result
of that preaching. When we look at how this word is used in the
Old Testament it paints a magnificent picture of the evangelist.

---

[29] *– (Gesenius, 2003)*

What Does an Evangelist Do?

*Isaiah 52:7-10 How lovely on the mountains Are the feet of him who **brings good news**, Who announces peace And brings **good news** of happiness, Who announces salvation, And says to Zion, "Your God reigns!" Listen! Your watchmen lift up their voices, They shout joyfully together; For they will see with their own eyes When the Lord restores Zion. Break forth, shout joyfully together, You waste places of Jerusalem; For the Lord has comforted His people, He has redeemed Jerusalem. The Lord has bared His holy arm In the sight of all the nations, That all the ends of the earth may see The salvation of our God.*

The evangelist:

- Brings good news
- Announces peace
- Announces salvation
- Proclaims the reign of God
- Shouts joyfully
- Proclaims the Lord's comfort upon His people
- Proclaims the Lord's redemption
- Proclaims the Lord's strength

I want to bring your attention to a particular phrase in that piece of Scripture. *"The Lord has bared His holy arm."* I am reminded of those moments in movies when a man is about to fight. He pulls up the sleeves of his shirt to intimidate his rival with the size of the muscles in his arm. The picture here is that God is baring His holy arm in the sight of all the nations so they might see how mighty He is and so they might behave in dealing with His children.

> ***Isaiah 40:9-11*** *Get yourself up on a high mountain, O Zion,* ***bearer of good news****, Lift up your voice mightily, O Jerusalem,* ***bearer of good news****; Lift it up, do not fear. Say to the cities of Judah, "Here is your God!" Behold, the Lord God will come with might, With His arm ruling for Him. Behold, His reward is with Him And His recompense before Him. Like a shepherd He will tend His flock, In His arm He will gather the lambs And carry them in His bosom; He will gently lead the nursing ewes.*

Here the evangelist:

- Is the bearer of good news
- Is to lift up their voice mightily
- Is not to fear
- Is to reveal God to the audience
- Is to declare the might of God
- Is to declare the gifts of God
- Is to declare the care of God

What a powerful call of God that lays within the evangelist!

> ***1 Chronicles 16:23-25*** *Sing to the Lord, all the earth; Proclaim* ***good tidings*** *of His salvation from day to day. Tell of His glory among the nations, His wonderful deeds among all the peoples. For great is the Lord, and greatly to be praised; He also is to be feared above all gods.*

The evangelist:

- Is to proclaim the good news of His salvation
- Is to tell of the glory of God
- Is to tell of God's wonderful deeds
- Is to proclaim praise unto God
- Is to proclaim the fear of God

Psalm 96:1-6 *Sing to the Lord a new song; Sing to the Lord, all the earth. Sing to the Lord, bless His name;* **Proclaim good tidings** *of His salvation from day to day.*

Tell of His glory among the nations, His wonderful deeds among all the peoples.

For great is the Lord and greatly to be praised; He is to be feared above all gods.

For all the gods of the peoples are idols, But the Lord made the heavens. Splendor and majesty are before Him, Strength and beauty are in His sanctuary.

The evangelist:

- Is to proclaim the good news of His salvation from day to day
- Is to proclaim the glory of God among the nations
- Is to proclaim the wonderful deeds among all the peoples
- Is to proclaim the greatness of the Lord
- Is to proclaim the fear of God
- Is to proclaim God as Creator
- Is to proclaim the majesty of God
- Is to proclaim the strength of God

- Is to proclaim the beauty of God

*Nahum 1:15 Behold, on the mountains the feet of him who **brings good news**, Who announces peace! Celebrate your feasts, O Judah; Pay your vows. For never again will the wicked one pass through you; He is cut off completely.*

As we have been going through the five callings, we have reiterated over and over that Jesus was all five callings in anointing, gifting, knowledge, and power. We have shown where Jesus was titled the Great Shepherd, the Apostle, that Prophet, and Master Teacher. However, as we have said, Jesus was never called the Evangelist. In the following Scriptures we will show Jesus the Evangelist.

Isaiah 61:1-3 The Spirit of the Lord God is upon me, Because the Lord has anointed me To bring good news to the afflicted; He has sent me to bind up the brokenhearted, To proclaim liberty to captives And freedom to prisoners; To proclaim the favorable year of the Lord And the day of vengeance of our God;

To comfort all who mourn, To grant those who mourn in Zion, Giving them a garland instead of ashes, The oil of gladness instead of mourning, The mantle of praise instead of a spirit of fainting. So they will be called oaks of righteousness,

The planting of the Lord, that He may be glorified.

Jesus, in Luke chapter four, read this section of Scripture in the synagogue and when He had finished, He sat down and said,

"Today this Scripture is fulfilled in your hearing." If we look carefully, we can see all five callings in that text.

"The Spirit of the Lord God is upon me, because the Lord has anointed me." No minister of Christ becomes a minister without the Spirit of the Lord being upon them. There will be those that claim the status of minister, but without the Spirit resting upon them they are no minister. Likewise, a person can call oneself a minister without the anointing, but God's true ministers walk in the anointing of the Holy Spirit.

"To bring good news to the afflicted;" – Here is **Evangelist Jesus** bringing *"evangeleon,"* the good news, to all of us afflicted with sin.

"He has sent me to bind up the brokenhearted," – Here is the **Apostle Jesus** for He is a *"sent one"* and is coming to fix that which is broken, to bring into order that which is out of order.

"To proclaim liberty to captives And freedom to prisoners;" – Here is the picture of **Teacher Jesus**. Jesus said that it was truth that sets us free and so the presentation of truth with understanding is the element that sets people free.

"To proclaim the favorable year of the Lord And the day of vengeance of our God;" – It is **Prophet Jesus** who proclaims the times and seasons of the moves of God in the earth. It is Prophet Jesus who declares the judgments of God.

"To comfort all who mourn, To grant those who mourn in Zion Giving them a garland instead of ashes, The oil of gladness instead of mourning, The mantle of praise instead of a spirit of fainting." – **Pastor** Jesus is seen here bringing comfort to His lambs. He is keeping them from fainting and He is anointing their heads with oil.

What is the purpose of the five fold ministry?

"So they will be called oaks of righteousness, the planting of the Lord, that He may be glorified." – It is to bring maturity to the Body of Christ, to bring unity of faith, to build up the Body. What a clear picture of our Lord and the gift ministries He has given the Church. This is in perfect agreement with Ephesians chapter four.

> ***Hebrews 10:5-9*** *Therefore, when He comes into the world, He says, "Sacrifice and offering You have not desired, But a body You have prepared for Me; In whole burnt offerings and sacrifices for sin You have taken no pleasure. Then I said, 'Behold, I have come (In the scroll of the book it is written of Me) To do Your will, O God.' " After saying above, "Sacrifices and offerings and whole burnt offerings and sacrifices for sin You have not desired, nor have You taken pleasure in them" (which are offered according to the Law), then He said, "Behold, I have come to do Your will." He takes away the first in order to establish the second.*

> ***Psalm 40:7-10*** *Then I said, "Behold, I come; In the scroll of the book it is written of me. I delight to do Your will, O my God; Your Law is within my heart." I have proclaimed **glad tidings** of righteousness in the great congregation; Behold, I will not restrain my lips, O Lord, You know. I have not hidden Your righteousness within my heart; I have spoken of Your faithfulness and Your salvation; I have not concealed Your lovingkindness and Your truth from the great congregation.*

Here again a section of Scripture that is associated with Jesus declares that He has proclaimed glad tidings of righteousness. This is the Evangelist Jesus. There should be no doubt at this point that Jesus was also the Evangelist.

How Would I Recognize This Calling in Myself or Others?

It should be clear to you that a strong desire for the proclamation of the Good News of the gospel of the kingdom is an indication of this calling. Those that hold the office of evangelist are focused on proclaiming that message. We have often put the emphasis on winning souls, but the Scripture puts the emphasis on proclaiming the Good News. The result of proclaiming the Good News is that souls are saved, but the evangelist should always have a first love of proclaiming that message!

What Kinds of Gifts Does the Evangelist Have?

One particular gift that stands out is the gift of exhortation. What is the gift of exhortation? The gift of exhortation is a gift that is used to motivate people to action in accordance with God's Word. It can be used in a one on one encounter or it can be used in preaching a sermon. The Greek word is *"parakaleo"* and it means *"to call to one's side."*

The picture is that of a person that is calling people to hear what they have to say. So this gift is the ability to preach in such a way that it draws people to hear. I have also witnessed that evangelists often are endowed with various gifts of healings. This is not necessarily so, but seems to be a common occurrence among those called to be an evangelist.

What Does an Evangelistic Church Look Like?

The evangelistic church will have a strong desire to proclaim the Good News to the lost. This means that because the lost do not normally come into a church there will be a diligent effort to send those that are saved into places where the unbeliever is to proclaim the Good News to the lost.

What is the Passion of the Evangelist?

The passion of the evangelist is consistent with proclaiming the Good News of the Kingdom of God. This means that they are very committed to preaching that message to the lost. They are often singularly driven to win souls through the preaching of that message.

Summing Up The Callings

Now that you have a good working knowledge of the five callings you should see there are passions that are very different depending on which calling you are looking at. This presents some problems for those that do not understand the government God intended for the Church. In Ephesians chapter four the Word states that *"HE gave..."* To whom did He give the five callings? It was to the Church for the equipping of the saints for the work of God.

Those who do not understand God's form of government are tempted to think that their passion is the right passion for the Church. They are right; their passion is the right passion, however, not to the exclusion of the other passions. God designed the council of His government to carry within it the five passions of the Person of Christ. If the other passions are missing from the Church, then a portion of God's passion for His people is missing in the demonstration of each calling.

This is why I hold diligently to the idea that each calling is not subservient to the others. What passion of Jesus is greater than the other? Which one can we do without? If we cannot separate, dissect, or devalue certain attributes of Christ, what makes us think that we can do so with the council who He called and through which He reveals Himself to the Church?

The church that functions like God has called it to function aligns itself to receive the manifest presence of God. When the tabernacle is complete the Spirit of God dwells in it. We have the inward dwelling of God in us as individuals; however, do we have the corporate presence of God that manifests itself corporately to the Church?

The Complete Church

The complete church desires to send people out, not only in the field of ministry to build new works, but also to send them out into the marketplace to take the kingdom of God into the varying components of society. She will be a place where the prophetic ministry is welcomed and encouraged. It is also a church that is highly focused in vision. There will be prophetic teaching, vision, dreams, prophetic evangelism, etc.

The complete church will be a teaching church. They will be a congregation that is able to defend outside the church what they believe to be true inside the church. They will be aware of the latest fads of false teachings. They will have a depth of knowledge concerning the doctrines of our faith. This will result in a congregation that is consistently taking what they are learning and making it a part of their life, producing a walk that is worthy of the Lord. They will also be aware of the different cults that are impacting the current culture.

She will have a strong desire to proclaim the Good News to the lost. This means that because the lost do not normally come into a church there will be a diligent effort to send those that are saved into places where the unbelievers are so they can proclaim the Good News to the lost. The complete church will be an empathetic church. Due to its empathy for others, it will have outreach programs to help the needy. It will focus on meeting basic physical needs of life. This church feels the needs of the community and will step up to meet those needs as best as it can.

The complete church not only cares for the physical needs of the community, but it will also care for their emotional needs. It will often be involved in one or more programs, such as help for alcoholics and drug addicts, single mother support, or battered women shelters and the like.

Can you imagine any part of that church being cut off and removed? No? Then you cannot cut off and remove any of the callings for those callings have a passion that is buried deep within the psyche and emotions of the individual that carries that calling. To cut them off is a disservice to the Body of Christ. Yet that is what we have done. We have cut off the prophet and apostle in some circles and we have cut out the pastor and teacher in other circles. We must accept the full council if we are to be a complete church.

The call of God is not to divide and compete, it is to unify and become a team. The weight of these words cannot be underscored. Am I willing to see the church down the road as a member of the team? Or do I look at them as the competition? If I am looking at the other churches in my neighborhood as the competition then who in the world is Satan? I thought our fight was with him. I thought that we were fighting to save a world that is fallen.

Much of the departure from teaching doctrine is the result of thinking that it (doctrine) is behind the division that has plagued God's people. Can we actually expect leaders to get along when they have different views on various doctrines? I think that we can agree that the primary doctrines of salvation must be adhered to by all groups if they are to be seen as Christian. On the other hand, I think there is room for discussion and dialogue on the others. For instance, I may not accept the eschatological leanings of the post trib teacher, but he is my brother and I can relate to him on that basis which actually opens up the atmosphere for dialogue.

We see that the early Church had their doctrinal disputes although they were not an occasion for division. They could disagree on issues and remain one Church. We have forgotten how to disagree as brothers. The council was to be a place where leaders would come together to hash out these doctrines and with the Holy Spirit leading, bring the Church into unity of belief. When the council was led by the Spirit, unity would result. This is why it is vital that the council be filled with men and women who are not in it for themselves, but are there for the good of the Church and the work of God.

One of the things that have plagued the Church for many years is the use of experiences in defining truths. We must resist the temptation to do such. Experiential knowledge is important, but can never be defining. I must never say this happened so God must… Instead we must always hold to what God said and intended in order to understand the experience. It is amazing how we can redefine an experience when we place it subservient to the Word of God.

Take Darwin for example. Many remember him for his work called "The Origin of the Species." However, many are not aware of the fact that Darwin was considered a theologian. How in the world could a theologian come to the place where they eliminate God from their own consciousness? It was an experience that caused Darwin to change his mind. Darwin had a daughter who died at a young age. The devastation of losing his child caused him to define God through his experience. By doing this, he concluded that God must not exist for he could not have allowed that kind of loss and pain if He did. This experience led to the conclusion that the origin of the species was of natural means rather than of creation. We know the devastating effect that work has had on the generations that have followed.

If Darwin would have looked at his experience through the eyes of the Word of God, he would have concluded that God's sovereign decision to allow his daughter to leave this world was an act of God's love. For Isaiah says the righteous are taken away and no one understands, but they are taken away from evil. Then in mourning the death of his daughter he could have thanked God that she was spared so much evil. The experience could have served to strengthen his relationship with God, rather than to ruin it.

Next, I want to share a prophetic message that God gave me for the Church. This message was a blueprint for restoration. If the Church is willing to walk in obedience, God will be willing to dwell in her.

Listen!

Chapter Eleven

Isaiah 48:1-2 ~NCV~
*The Lord says, "Family of Jacob, **listen to me.** You
are called Israel, and you come from the family of
Judah. **You swear by the Lord's name and praise
the God of Israel, but you are not honest or
sincere. You call yourselves people of the holy
city**, and you depend on the God of Israel, who is
named the Lord All-Powerful.*

G od is doing different things at different times with His
Church. There are seasons and times that God sanctions
for His people. But if we will not listen, if we will not
move, we come out of step with God. His people have a tendency
of getting comfortable in the way of the past and are unwilling to
move into the things He is doing today.

Satan is the god of this age. That means that he constantly
changes his strategy with each generation. If the Church is
unwilling to keep in step with God they will no longer be ahead of
the enemy's plans, but behind them. The danger in getting behind
the enemy is that you lose relevance. Relevance is important with
regard to communicating with the current culture. If you lose it,
you lose the ability to communicate to the culture and become
irrelevant to it.

Once you lose your voice in the culture it is very difficult to
get it back. When I scan the culture of America, I am saddened by
the fact that the Church has lost her voice because she has gotten
out of step with the King of kings and the Lord of lords.

Isaiah 48:3-5 ~NCV~

*Long ago I told you what would happen. I said
these things and made them known; suddenly I
acted, and these things happened. I knew you were
stubborn; your neck was like an iron muscle, and
your head was like bronze. So a long time ago I told
you about these things; I told you about them before
they happened so you couldn't say, 'My idols did
this, and my wooden and metal statues made these
things happen.'*

One of the things that will mark an irrelevant Church is that they will rely upon their idols. What idols? The idols of systems and traditions that have made God's word ineffective. Churches have a tendency to do what works rather than what God is saying. You can get a large congregation if you entertain them enough, but what do they become?

When God tells one generation to do something a certain way, the next generation makes it into a system or formula for success. We need to be a people that seek a fresh Word from God. A people that would be willing to hear what the Spirit is saying to the people. I don't want to do church like the previous generation unless the Spirit says so. God help us to become a people with a voice in the earth!

Isaiah 48:6-8 ~NCV~

*"You heard and saw everything that happened, so
you should tell this news to others. Now I will tell
you about **new** things, hidden things that you don't
know yet. These things are happening now, not long
ago; you have not heard about them before today.
So you cannot say, 'We already knew about that.'*

***But you have not heard me; you have not understood.** Even long ago you did not listen to me. I knew you would surely turn against me; you have fought against me since you were born.*

God is speaking. He is giving directions for us. He wants to do a new thing. He will not change His Word, but He does change His tactics. Are we hearing them, are we understanding them. Or are we so proud we, too, would say, **"I knew that!"**

How many times have ministers and congregations held onto the past way of doing things, became introspective, then isolated, then dead? If we are going to be a force in this earth we have to stay fresh and up to date with the Spirit. We have to engage the culture and the spirit of this age, contending with their beliefs and philosophies by showing them the relevance of the Word of God to their condition.

Isaiah 48:12-15 ~NCV~
*12 "People of Jacob, **listen to me**. People of Israel, I have called you to be my people. I am God; I am the beginning and the end.*

13 I made the earth with my own hands. With my right hand I spread out the skies.

When I call them, they come together before me."

*14 All of you, **come together and listen.** None of the gods said these things would happen. The Lord has chosen someone to attack the Babylonians; he will carry out his wishes against Babylon.*

15 "I have spoken; I have called him. I have brought him, and I will make him successful.

I keep hearing the Spirit shout **"LISTEN!"** Why won't the people of God listen? The stars come together when God calls them, but not His people. We should be seeking the face of God until He answers us with a fresh and relevant move of His Spirit.

God has called you, He has brought you near to Him, and if you will listen He will make you successful. Sometimes I feel like we need to make an 1800 year leap. Why? It was 1800 years ago when the Church quit discipling. Only those who the Church thought were called to a pulpit ministry were discipled. God wants a smart Church, an intelligent Church. He wants a Church who can give an answer for the hope that lies within them.

> ### Isaiah 48:16-19 ~NCV~
> *16 Come to me and **listen** to this. From the beginning I have spoken openly. From the time it began, I was there." Now, the Lord God has sent me with his Spirit.*
>
> *17 This is what the Lord, who saves you, the Holy One of Israel, says: "I am the Lord your God, who **teaches you** to do what is good, **who leads you in the way you should go.***
>
> *18 If you **had obeyed me**, you would have had peace like a full-flowing river. Good things would have flowed to you like the waves of the sea.*
>
> *19 You would have had many children, as many as the grains of sand. They would never have died out nor been destroyed."*

If we would but hear Him and do according to His leading, we would be in safety and prosperity. Our congregations would have been many. They would not have left us and gone back to the world. We think we are sacrificing by holding on to the past ways.

God seeks obedience! God is not changing His Church structure and He is not changing His government. He is, however, changing His tactics. He is always way ahead of the enemy.

> **Zechariah 7:8-11**
> *8 Then the word of the Lord came to Zechariah saying,*
>
> *9 "Thus has the Lord of hosts said, 'Dispense true justice and practice kindness and compassion each to his brother;*
>
> *10 and do not oppress the widow or the orphan, the stranger or the poor; and do not devise evil in your hearts against one another.'*
>
> **11 "But they refused to pay attention and turned a stubborn shoulder and stopped their ears from hearing.**

Have we refused to pay attention to what God is saying now? Have we turned a stubborn shoulder and stopped our ears from hearing? Hearing God is not optional. If you refuse to hear Him you become incapable of hearing Him. Do you understand this? You literally place upon yourself a self inflicted deafness.

> **Zechariah 7:12** *"They made their hearts like flint so that they **could not hear** the law and the words which the Lord of hosts had sent by His Spirit through the former prophets; therefore great wrath came from the Lord of hosts.*

When a person walks willfully into rebellion by refusing to hear the Word of God, whether it is His written Word or a Word spoken by the Spirit of God, they suddenly cannot hear from God. I have seen this happen so many times. We have had students who suddenly are unable to pass a test or write a report. Upon inspection of them we find that they walked into rebellion. They become "dumb" because they have set their heart against something God has said.

People actually think they can do what they want without any consequence. What do you think God will do when you refuse to hear Him? Do you think He just becomes indifferent to it? He does not. He will deal with you until you decide to turn around and come back.

> **Zechariah 7:13-14 "And just as He called and they would not listen, so they called and I would not listen," says the Lord of hosts;** *"but I scattered them with a storm wind among all the nations whom they have not known. Thus the land is desolated behind them so that no one went back and forth, for they made the pleasant land desolate."*

How is it that we expect God to listen to us when we are unwilling to listen to Him? You wonder why the heavens are brass when you try to pray. Rebellion comes in many different shapes and flavors. You might be tempted to think you are not in rebellion when you are.

Do you read God's Word and accept only part of it? You are in rebellion. Have you refused counsel from those God has set over you? You are in rebellion. Are you refusing to participate in the Body of Christ? You are in rebellion.

> **Jeremiah 35:15 ~NCV~** *I sent all my servants the prophets to you again and again, saying, "Each of you must stop doing evil. You must change and be good. Do not follow other gods to serve them. If you obey me, you will live in the land I have given to*

you and your ancestors." **But you have not listened to me or paid attention to my message.**

The nation of Israel had become worshipers of Baal. Even today in what we call the Church there are many who are worshiping another god. They make gods to suit themselves. They make gods that would agree with their philosophy and their lifestyle.

What follows is what the Lord revealed to me is the pattern in which He will deal with His people and what they must do to be restored. The Lord will not let His people wander to other gods without dealing with them.

Rebuilding the Altar of the Lord

1 Kings 18:30-48

> *Verse 30 Then Elijah said to all the people, "Come near to me." So all the people came near to him. And he **repaired the altar of the Lord** which had been torn down.*

What is an altar? The root word in Hebrew means "to kill." Whose altar is it? It is the altar of the Lord. It is where man meets God and realizes that the holiness of God demands man's sacrifice. The altar is where we find Christ, the One who was offered up as a sacrifice for us. In order for the Church to be restored we must repair this altar. As I consider the altar of the Lord, I am faced with the fact that Jesus was here before me, yet He invites me to slay my life upon that altar; to be willing to give my life and will to Him for His perfect purpose to be lived out in me.

The altar does not only mean our sacrifice, but it represents the image of God. We cannot come to the altar and see the necessity of sacrifice without first beholding Him who calls us to it. Without that vision of God, we will not see a need for the killing of self interest. **Therefore, if the Church is to be restored we must repair God's image into the same One He revealed to His creation.** This is represented by rebuilding the altar of the Lord.

Man in all of his attempts at self sufficiency is sorely unprepared for living a life fully dependant on the Son of Righteousness. However, the altar demands that what I bring to it is insufficient compared to what I take from it. What I lay upon it is all of my ability, intelligence, and talent. I take from it the power of the Son to be the Body of Him and behold His work through my hands and feet. The rebuilding of the altar, however, is a process.

Restore Identity

> **Verse 31** *Elijah took twelve stones according to the number of the tribes of the sons of Jacob, to whom the word of the Lord had come, saying,* **"Israel shall be your name."**

Why did Elijah need to take twelve stones and then say *"Israel shall be your name?"* The people of Israel had forgotten their identity! So also, the Church has forgotten her identity. The first step then in rebuilding the altar of the Lord is to revitalize our identity in Him. Note that identity is only possible when you merge with another.

You cannot produce identity yourself. If you attempt to, you will only succeed in producing individualism. You will make an image of yourself, but that image is your building. Identity is who you really are. That can only be found through merging with the Creator of who you really are. If you are created in His image you will need to find Him to find yourself.

Build With Identity

> *Verse 32 So **with the stones he built an altar** in the name of the Lord, and he made a trench around the altar, large enough to hold two measures of seed.*

Once Elijah reveals the identity of Israel, he begins to build the altar of the Lord with it. What God has done in the earth since Adam has always been a partnership between man and God, but man without identity is a wanderer. I have witnessed many in the kingdom of God who wander aimlessly through life. They have not restored true identity. It is impossible to build the work of God without first knowing who you are through mergence with Jesus your Creator.

Look at the patterns in the Bible. Moses was not able to enter the fullness of his ministry until he realized who God was which gave him the epiphany of who he was. It took a burning bush for Moses.

Jacob was not able to enter the fullness of his ministry until he realized who God was which gave him the epiphany of who he was. It took wrestling with God for Jacob and the discovery of a new name (Israel) revealed the true identity of the man.

For us, it is the cross. For when we look upon that old rugged cross we see our Creator who died for us, we see our inadequacy, failures, and sins. Then as we see the face of the suffering Savior, we merge with Him and He with us. Then we are free to see ourselves, our true identity, and at that moment we are set free to be and live a fruitful life.

Sustain the Sacrifice

> *Verse 33 Then he arranged the wood and cut the ox in pieces and laid it on the wood.*

Wood is necessary to sustain the fire to consume the sacrifice. Wood also sustained the sacrifice for the whole world. The sacrifice was laid upon the wood. One can hardly bear the thought of our Savior, our Creator being, laid upon the wood of the cross as three spikes were driven through His hands and feet.

Do not forget that Jesus was also cut in pieces before He was laid upon the cross. He had endured the beatings and the whippings that would cause His flesh to be flayed in strips. Then He was hoisted upright to be displayed as a piece of meat in the market place.

Rebuilding the altar means that a sacrifice must be offered. That sacrifice might not take the form of a bloody corpse, but it should take the form of a tattered and bloody soul ready to give its all for the glory of God. What form that sacrifice takes after it is offered is akin to the resurrected Lord who shined with the brightness of the glory of God.

Saturate the Sacrifice

> **Verse 34-35** *And he said, "Fill four pitchers with water and pour it on the burnt offering and on the wood." And he said, "Do it a second time," and they did it a second time. And he said, "Do it a third time," and they did it a third time. The water flowed around the altar and he also filled the trench with water.*

Water speaks of the Word of God; both the Logos and the Rhema. Note that this water saturated the ground around the altar with the sacrifice upon it. The rebuilding of the altar cannot be completed without the Word of God being put in a place of preeminence in the life of the Christian. We must saturate ourselves with the Word of God.

The restoration of the Church will not happen without an awakening to the Word of God. When the Bible has been placed below praise and worship or programs, the Church is weakened into becoming anemic and ineffective. Renew the fervor that we once had for the Word!

Make a Declaration of Sacrifice

> *Verses 36-37 At the time of the offering of the evening sacrifice, Elijah the prophet came near and said, "O Lord, the God of Abraham, Isaac and Israel, today let it be known that You are God in Israel and that I am Your servant and I have done all these things at Your word. "Answer me, O Lord, answer me, that this people may know that You, O Lord, are God, and that **You have turned their heart back again.**"*

The last step in rebuilding the altar of the Lord is to make a declaration of faith. We must make a declaration and a prayer to God:

"O Lord, the God of Abraham, Isaac and Israel, today let it be known that You are God in my house and that we are Your servants and we have done all these things at Your word. Answer us, O Lord, answer us, that this people may know that You, O Lord are God, and that You have turned their heart back again."

Fire will Fall

> *Verses 38-39 Then the **fire of the Lord fell** and consumed the burnt offering and the wood and the stones and the dust, and licked up the water that was in the trench. When all the people saw it, they*

fell on their faces; and they said, "The Lord, He is God; the Lord, He is God."

If we will rebuild the altar prescribed in this manner, then the fire of God will fall on the Church. Just remember that God is a consuming fire. Something will be consumed. Self image, self interest, self indulgence, and self will be consumed. If we will do this with our life, then others will see it, fall on their face and say, *"The Lord, He is God; the Lord, He is God."*

The Result

> ***Verse 40*** *Then Elijah said to them, "Seize the prophets of Baal; do not let one of them escape." So they seized them; and Elijah brought them down to the brook Kishon, and slew them there.*

Once we have rebuilt the altar of the Lord in our lives and in our churches, then and only then will we be able to confront the false philosophies with the truth. Once confronted, we will need to seize the moment and put to death those philosophies that caused the people of God to fashion gods to suit themselves. When we take our place, God will also silence those false prophets that only prophecy peace and safety.

> ***Micah 3:5-8 ~NCV~***
> *5 The Lord says this about the prophets who teach his people the wrong way of living: "If these prophets are given food to eat, they shout, 'Peace!' But if someone doesn't give them what they ask for, they call for a holy war against that person.*
>
> *6 So it will become like night for them, without visions. It will become dark for them, without any*

way to tell the future. The sun is about to set for the prophets; their day will become dark.

7 The seers will be ashamed; the people who see the future will be embarrassed. Yes, all of them will cover their mouths, because there will be no answer from God."

8 But I am filled with power, with the Spirit of the Lord, and with justice and strength, to tell the people of Jacob how they have turned against God, and the people of Israel how they have sinned.

If we will stay true to what God is doing, we will be able to say like Micah, *"I am filled with power, with the Spirit of the Lord, and with justice and strength, to tell the people of God how they have turned against God, and the people of God how they have sinned."* You will be able to contend with those inside the Church to rebuild their altars. Not all will hear and do, but you will be able to reach some of them.

Jeremiah 6:16 ~NCV~ *This is what the Lord says: "Stand where the roads cross and look. Ask where the old way is, where the good way is, and walk on it. If you do, you will find rest for yourselves. But they have said, 'We will not walk on the good way.'*

We are at our crossroads! Two ways are presented to us; both of them are to be heeded. One is "the old way." This represents the Laws and nature of God. These things never change, they are always the same. We are encouraged to look for this and walk in it. Then there is "the good way." The good way represents entering into what God is doing today.

So we must look for the attributes of God that never change and find the will of God for today. This means that since you have rebuilt the altar of the Lord and you have laid yourself upon it, you are now ready to enter into your destiny.

> ### *Jeremiah 6:17-19 ~NCV~*
> *17 I set watchmen over you and told you, '**Listen** for the sound of the war trumpet!' But they said, 'We will not listen.'*
>
> *18 So listen, all you nations, and pay attention, you witnesses. Watch what I will do to the people of Judah.*
>
> *19 Hear this, **people of the earth**: I am going to bring disaster to the people of Judah because of the evil they plan. They have not listened to my messages and have rejected my teachings.*

God revealed to me that the people of the earth are waiting for the people of God to catch up to what He is doing. They can see it, but they cannot enter in without God's people leading the way. They will not move until the people of God come into the same frequency that He is operating on. God wants us to be in resonance with His Spirit.

> ### *"QUOTE"*
> *Resonance: The increase in amplitude of oscillation of an electric or mechanical system exposed to a periodic force whose frequency is equal or very close to the natural undamped frequency of the system. **To relate harmoniously**. a synchronous gravitational relationship of two celestial bodies*

When we do what God is doing, we come into the same frequency He is using. It will then produce a resonance that will cause the people of the world to be able to hear the Words of God.

Proverbs 1:20-33

28 "Then they will call on me, but I will not answer;
They will seek me diligently but they will not find
me,

*29 **Because they hated knowledge** And did not*
choose the fear of the Lord.

30 They would not accept my counsel, They spurned
all my reproof.

31 So they shall eat of the fruit of their own way
And be satiated with their own devices.

*32 **For the waywardness of the naive will kill them,***
And the complacency of fools will destroy them.

33 But he who listens to me shall live securely And
will be at ease from the dread of evil."

What does it mean to listen to God? Is it only His Word, or
is it more? How do I enter into the promise of living securely?
When God has given us extra biblical instructions, is that added to
the condition of "he who listens to me?"

Indeed! If we refuse His instructions, whether He speaks
them into your spirit or they come through prophetic ministry, are
meant to be followed. Note that I am talking about a legitimate
prophetic word spoken by the Holy Spirit. There have been a lot of
words spoken over individuals that are nothing more than
divination. God knows that we would be at this time in history.
Apostle Paul had this problem during his time, to which he wrote:

__1 Thessalonians 5:20-21__ do not despise prophetic utterances. But examine everything carefully; hold fast to that which is good...

We must examine every prophetic word carefully and hold fast to that which is good.

__Revelation 2:7__ 'He who has an ear, let him hear what the Spirit says to the churches. To him who overcomes, I will grant to eat of the tree of life which is in the Paradise of God.'

Not every person has an ear that can hear what the Spirit of God is saying. Only those who are of the household of faith whose spirit has been born again with the Spirit of God will be able to hear. In other words, you were born to hear God - so listen!

__John 3:8__ "The wind blows where it wishes and __you hear the sound of it__, but do not know where it comes from and where it is going; so is everyone who is born of the Spirit."

We are born of the Spirit and we can hear the wind of the Spirit. If we will hear the wind of the Spirit then we can operate in perfect step with God and produce an outcome that will result in the fire of God falling upon His people. You can hear it! You may not know where it is coming from or where it is going, but you can hear it. Tune your ear to hear the voice of the Spirit.

__John 16:13__ "But when He, the Spirit of truth, comes, He will guide you into all the truth; for He will not speak on His own initiative, but whatever He hears, He will speak; and __He will disclose to you what is to come.__"

Wait a minute! The Holy Spirit will disclose to you what is to come? You mean the future? What I am supposed to do? Yes! God wants us to be part of His strategic plan upon this earth. He wants us to be a force against evil. He wants us to know what He is doing. He wants us to be His voice in the earth!

> **Revelation 22:17** *The Spirit and the bride say, "Come." And let the one who hears say, "Come." And let the one who is thirsty come; let the one who wishes take the water of life without cost.*

This is very important to understand. God wants His Church to be in step with what He is doing. He does not want us stuck in programs, systems, formulas, or the past. This is the revelation of this verse. **When we are in sync with the Spirit; when we are saying what the Spirit is saying, then, and only then, will the world be able to hear our voice!**

About the Author

Bishop Mark Shaw and his wife Kathryn, are co-founders and directors of *Five Fold Ministries Training Academy (FFMTA)* and *Collegium Bible Institute* where the next generation of ministers is being equipped for God's service around the world. Bishop Shaw is the author of *"Is God Calling You to Ministry?"* and *"The Glory of Kings."* Shaw is the senior editor of *A Voice in the Wilderness* newsletter, which is published quarterly. He is also founder of Collegium Books, which is a publishing and distribution firm that seeks to offer educational materials for the equipping of the saints for the work of God. Shaw has been in ministry for thirty-two years. He was vice-director of Five Fold Ministries for twelve years and has been director for the last nine years. He also presides as pastor over *Adonai Worship Center* in Cannon Falls, Minnesota.

Shaw teaches on the structure and government of the Church with emphasis on divine order. He brings clarity to the Scripture by revealing a Hebraic understanding and emphasizes the causes and conditions upon which we develop our faith. His desire is to return true discipleship back to the Church so that true leaders are being forged with truth and integrity. He has a vision for the Church that is cutting edge and Spirit mandated.

In 2008 Shaw founded the Five Fold Ministries on-line E-learning center. The E-learning center is designed to distribute world class learning to students through internet technology that brings the school into the living room. The purpose is to develop leaders nationally and internationally that are willing to arrange the Church and its leaders in such a way that validates the Church as a voice in a secular society.

Called to the office of ministry, Kathryn Colton Shaw has a heart and a voice to teach those that are hungry to walk in the ways of the Lord, and awaken them to do what God has called them to do. It is Kathryn's desire to bring healing to the whole person in order that they may be released to accomplish the destiny for which they were created. Kathryn has a gift for networking and hosting seminars and educational programs. She is also gifted in administration and is a valuable asset in giving direction to the Church. Pastor Kathryn is the co-founder of *FFMTA* and *Collegium Bible Institute* where she serves as Academic Dean/Counselor and continues to develop curriculum to impact the next generation for Christ. The Shaws reside in Minnesota and they have six children and ten grandchildren that live in California and North Carolina.

Collegium Bible Institute

The International Equipping School of the Five Fold Ministry

Collegium Bible Institute is a four year biblical institute where students are prepared for ministry and receive a deep sense of awe for the Scriptures. For more information on our ordination program at the local campus, write us at 410 Dakota Street W, Cannon Falls, MN 55009 or call us at 888-808-5455. Our website is: www.collegiumbibleinstitute.com

If you are interested in the Online E-Learning Center visit us at: www.5fold.org.

The Lord commanded His disciples to go into all the world and make disciples of all nations, teaching them to observe all that He said. The question then is have you been discipled yet?

Coming in January 2010

"What you believe to be true will create responses that result in actions; when they are lies, your responses are acts of bondage"

Warfare!
Strategies of the Enemy

Mark David Shaw
Kathryn Colton Shaw

IS GOD CALLING
YOU TO MINISTRY?

*Get Ready to Discover
Your Purpose and
Step Into Your
Destiny*

Mark David Shaw

Five Fold Ministries
Destiny Series

Available Now on Amazon.com!

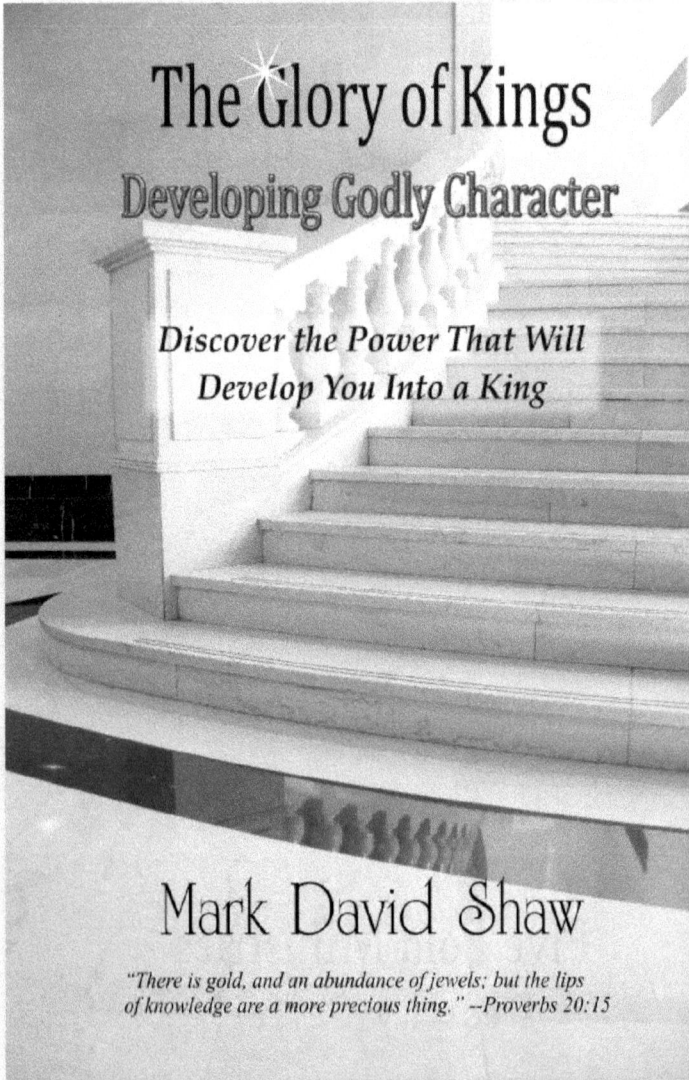

The Glory of Kings
Developing Godly Character

Discover the Power That Will
Develop You Into a King

Mark David Shaw

"There is gold, and an abundance of jewels; but the lips
of knowledge are a more precious thing." --Proverbs 20:15

www.ingramcontent.com/pod-product-compliance
Lightning Source LLC
Chambersburg PA
CBHW070344090426
42733CB00009B/1280